Conception and Installation of System Monito using the SAP Solution Manager

Corina Schulz

Contents

Contents

Introduction

Due to the growing use of newly developed system components, system landscapes are becoming increasingly more complex. These system components constitute not only SAP systems, but applications outside the SAP world as well. For the IT staff of a company, this means that they constantly have to enhance their knowledge of the administration and monitoring of these different system environments. Generally, the responsibility for training the staff and empowering them with such knowledge rests with a few employees, since not everyone can be an expert in every area. This leads to the situation whereby knowledge is organized decentrally. With regard to system monitoring, you can safely say that every expert does a very good job in his or her specific area of expertise. Therefore, due to the decentral organization of the specialist areas within the IT department, the degree of quality is high, but it comes at a price—the expenditure in time for system monitoring. This expenditure can be reduced by automating and centralizing the monitoring process of heterogeneous system landscapes, which should be the objective of any company.

In the past two years, customers often asked me questions about centralized system monitoring. And many times I was asked the same questions, such as: What do we have to monitor within our SAP solution? Which technical components of our system landscape will be monitored? Which performance-relevant components could be used for proactive system monitoring? Which specific areas of an SAP solution, such as Advanced Planning and Optimization (APO), should be integrated into the monitoring process? Which monitoring application would you recommend? What kind of monitoring tools are provided by SAP? How can you monitor a heterogeneous system landscape with SAP tools? Which system monitoring functions does SAP Solution Manager provide? How does system monitoring work within SAP Solution Manager?

These and other questions contributed to my getting a rather comprehensive overview of the current state of system monitoring processes in various companies. For example, there were IT departments in which people were fully aware of the importance of system monitoring. However, due to a limited number of staff, they had never been able to implement traditional system monitoring processes. They simply didn't have the time to do it. Other companies felt that centralized system monitoring wasn't necessary, because they thought their system landscapes weren't that complex. In such cases, I could only tell them that—in time—system landscapes would become increasingly complex, and the sooner they started implementing a monitoring system, the less effort they would need to integrate new systems into the monitoring process. But there were also companies that seriously considered implementing a centralized system monitoring process as a result of a complete system failure during business hours. They could have avoided a lot of trouble if a monitoring process had been implemented for at least some areas, for example, system performance.

The knowledge I gathered in the field of system monitoring, as well as the continuous enhancements made to SAP Solution Manager, now serve as a basis for me to introduce you to a great deal of general information about centralized system monitoring with SAP Solution Manager as your monitoring tool. Therefore, I tackled this challenge and wrote down my experiences in this specific area for you. My colleagues, Jens-Fischer, Marko Schmidt, and Uwe Wenzel, who have been involved in the development of SAP Solution Manager since its inception, have added a great deal of useful information about the application, in particular, for the practical part of this book. I would also like to thank Liane Will, Vital Anderhub, Rüdiger Stökker, Mathias Melich, and Cay Rademann for their invaluable support.

Contents of this Book

This book will provide you with information that facilitates the conceptual design and implementation of a centralized system monitoring. You'll get an overview of the aspects that are integral to the design phase of your monitoring system. The design phase is followed by the implementation, which is supported by the use of SAP Solution Manager.

As a welcome departure from pure theory, a sample scenario will accompany you throughout this book. This sample scenario describes the system landscape of Toys Inc., a fictitious company. Based on the initial situation of this company, you will see step by step how a decentralized system monitoring process will be converted into a centralized one.

Target Audience

This book addresses those readers who administer and monitor both SAP systems and systems outside of the SAP environment. Those who are currently on the lookout for an appropriate monitoring tool for their own system landscape are also invited to reflect on the following chapters. Perhaps you will find yourself in a situation whereby you have to implement a centralized system monitoring model, and therefore can use this book as the basis for the selection of the relevant monitoring objects.

Presuppositions

To fully understand the contents of this book, you should have experience in the administration of SAP systems and non-SAP system components. Furthermore, you should be familiar with the specific SAP terminology and that of other related areas. Last, it will prove advantageous if you're familiar with the SAP monitoring architecture Computing Center Management System (CCMS).

Contents of the Individual Chapters

In **Chapter 1**, we'll describe the fundamental reasons why centralized system monitoring has advantages over a decentralized approach. Apart from this, we will introduce SAP Solution Manager as an appropriate monitoring tool and explain which requirements must be fulfilled in order to achieve a successful implementation of centralized monitoring. In this context, you will also find some basic information on the design of a monitoring concept. As we already mentioned, we'll always refer to Toys Inc., whose initial system monitoring concept will be described in the first chapter.

Chapter 2 provides you with a comprehensive overview of the functionality of SAP Solution Manager. We'll describe various ways to integrate and use SAP Solution Manager in your system landscape. You'll be introduced to SAP Solution Manager as an implementation platform, a solution monitoring platform, a service provider platform, as a service channel to SAP Service Marketplace, a documentation platform, and as a service desk platform.

Before you set up system monitoring within SAP Solution Manager, you should consider which system components and modules to include in the monitoring process. These considerations are discussed in **Chapter 3**, which deals with the creation of a monitoring concept. The monitoring concept will include selected monitoring objects such as system availability and R/3 buffer settings.

In **Chapter 4**, you will learn how system monitoring can be configured and mapped for a specific system landscape in SAP Solution Manager. A series of screenshots will guide you through SAP Solution Manager in this chapter. To give you a practical and concrete overview of the functional scope of system monitoring, we'll demonstrate the navigation on the basis of the fictitious system landscape of our sample company, Toys Inc.

SAP Solution Manager Release 3.1 will serve as the basis when we set up the system monitoring. All the menu paths and names specified here refer to this release. Please note that in other releases (for example, 2.1, 2.2, or 3.2), the interface and navigation paths might not correspond to those in Release 3.1.

1 The Problem and a Sample Scenario

In this chapter, we'll lay the foundation for the monitoring concept used throughout the book. We'll discuss the advantages of centralized monitoring over decentralized monitoring, describe the basic functions of SAP Solution Manager, and outline the sample scenario for our concept.

1.1 Centralized and Decentralized System Monitoring

The following criteria describe which aspects should be considered when you decide to implement centralized or decentralized system monitoring. These are fundamental operational values, not a technical laundry list, so think of this as an opportunity to ask yourself which kind of monitoring is optimal for your company.

▶ **Time**

Time and efficiency are interdependent. Every company strives to use the capacity of its employees in such a way that there is a balanced relationship between the utility of their activities and the underlying effort. If a highly qualified IT administrator spends most of his or her working hours monitoring systems, this might be important for a smooth system operation; however, for the company, this is not efficient. Therefore, if you consider all the specialists in the IT department who are responsible for system monitoring, it is far better to centrally bundle the working time that each individual otherwise would spend on monitoring his or her specific area.

▶ **Technical expertise**

A person who specializes in a certain area of expertise for which he or she is responsible in a decentralized model would probably achieve better results in this area than someone who monitors the entire system landscape. However, such knowledge and exper-

tise can be integrated in a centralized monitoring concept that focuses only on the essential aspects of system monitoring. You define a certain number of monitoring objects and threshold values. That is to say, based on your own experience, you specify the values that tell you when a problem is about to occur within a system or when you have to act in order to ensure a continued system operation.

▶ **Single Point of Access**

Suppose someone asks you:

- ▶ Which systems you monitor
- ▶ Where most of the system problems occur
- ▶ Which is the current release of the systems in use
- ▶ Which SAP and non-SAP systems you are currently using
- ▶ Which parts of the systems you think could be optimized
- ▶ If you have adhered to the service level agreements (SLAs) with other business partners (for example, of the application) in the past five months

Of course, in a decentralized system monitoring model, you can easily ask the relevant people to get a comprehensive overview of all of the above. But what would you do if someone wanted you to answer on the spot? Wouldn't it be much nicer to administer and monitor your system information as a whole? Or rather, wouldn't it be great to have just one single point of access to all the information you need?

▶ **Communication interfaces**

Both the decentralized and the centralized system monitoring contain communication interfaces. In the centralized monitoring model, the number of interfaces can be greater than in the decentralized model because more people may be involved in the monitoring process. For example, there is an additional interface between the person who monitors the systems and the person referred to in the event of a problem. However, you should keep in mind that many interfaces can affect the total system performance.

▶ **Monitoring additional system components**
In these times—when new software components and technologies enter the market evermore rapidly—the shape of a system landscape changes accordingly. In order to keep up with this pace and keep track of which system and application components are or will be included in the system monitoring process, a centralized system monitoring model offers great benefits.

All the criteria listed above support the implementation of a centralized model. Due to efficient time management and a clear definition of tasks, centralized system monitoring enables you to minimize or even avoid negative financial effects for a company after a failure of its IT systems. In this context, monitoring activities are automated and processes are defined, which are necessary for system monitoring and troubleshooting.

Therefore, IT specialists, such as the database expert, are much better equipped to focus on their core areas of expertise and simultaneously study other areas. This affords them the freedom to familiarize themselves with new technologies, which results in a further optimization of the stability and performance of their systems.

The centralized character of the monitoring process moves the collaboration of different application components in a heterogeneous system landscape into the focus of interest. The interactions and the consequences of system problems existing between different application components are important in a heterogeneous system landscape within the centralized system monitoring. No longer are individual system objects regarded as separate entities; it is much more important to see the interaction between these objects and to discover which interdependencies exist between them if a failure occurs at a certain point within the system.

1.2   SAP Solution Manager

SAP Solution Manager is a software developed by SAP. It is the central platform that provides efficient support for your SAP system landscape—both in the implementation phase and during operation.

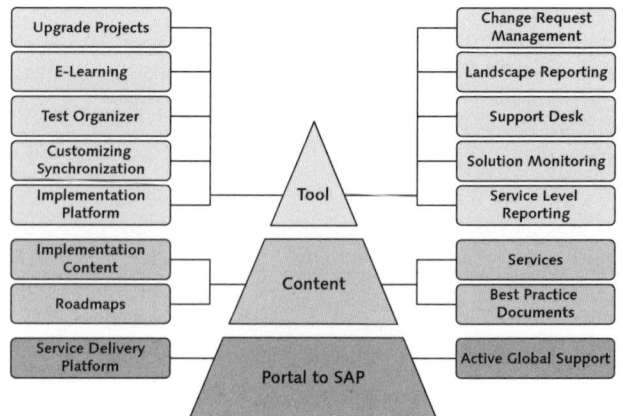

Figure 1.1 SAP Solution Manager as the Central Platform of a Solution Landscape

Portal

With SAP Solution Manager, you have a portal at your disposal that enables you to directly connect to *SAP Service Marketplace* and *SAP Support*. SAP Solution Manager enables you to quickly and easily order the services provided by SAP. For example, if there is a problem with your system's performance and you urgently need an analysis, you can send a service order from the SAP Solution Management Optimization program in SAP Solution Manager. The service can then be run within SAP Solution Manager. The link to SAP Service Marketplace also enables you to have direct access to SAP Active Global Support and the SAP Notes that will be provided via the SAP Solution Manager in the event of a problem.

Content

The second function is the so-called content. SAP Solution Manager provides you with extensive knowledge gathered by consultants and support staff in the course of customer projects.

Predefined *Project phases* are available to you, which are intended to facilitate the implementation of business processes. For example, if you want to integrate a Supply Chain Management (SCM) system or another mySAP Business Suite solution into your system landscape, you'll find predefined process and configuration descriptions in SAP Solution Manager just for this purpose.

In addition, SAP Solution Manager contains *Documentation* that is required for your system landscape. This means that when you run both an R/3 system and an SCM system, documentation for these components is automatically provided in SAP Solution Manager. Documentation can be Best Practices, which focus on one specific subject within an SAP component; for example, the liveCache Backup and Recovery provides necessary know-how in order to run an SCM system. These documents are written by experienced SAP support employees.

Apart from the components already described, SAP Solution Manager also provides *Roadmaps*. A roadmap is a guideline for an upgrade project. You learn step by step what you have to consider during an upgrade project and in which order the steps are to be carried out.

As you already know, SAP offers various *Services* in the context of its support activities. These services include SAP EarlyWatch Check, SAP GoingLive Check, SAP Remote Performance Optimization, SAP Solution Management Optimization Services, and all of these services can be run in SAP Solution Manager.

Tool

SAP Solution Manager supports you during the entire lifecycle of your solutions. In other words, as soon as new solutions are introduced, SAP Solution Manager provides you with an *Implementation platform*. This platform provides tools and methods within SAP Solution Manager to which you have a centralized access during the complete period of implementation—from the business blueprint via configuration to the final implementation. Centralized storage of the project documentation within SAP Solution Manager enables you to quickly access all your project information.

A tool that compares the customizing objects of a system in an SAP system landscape with customizing objects in SAP R/3 is the so-called *Customizing Synchronization*. For example, you can compare the customizing of a mySAP SCM with that of SAP R/3. You should use this tool to avoid differing customizing settings in the individual SAP components. By comparing the settings or the specific customizing objects with each other, you can keep them in sync.

It is an essential part of every project to perform testing on a newly implemented solution. You can organize and perform tests at certain project stages by using the *Test Organizer*. To do this, you create test plans or test packages for individual testers in SAP Solution Manager; status information on the progress of such tests can be retrieved at any time.

After the implementation of a new solution and the new functions that go with it, the users need to get trained. You can use *E-Learning* in SAP Solution Manager to create learning maps from existing project structures. These learning maps are available to the user at any time and contain an overview of functions that a user needs to perform his or her tasks within the new system solution.

If you plan to upgrade one or more SAP components, the very convenient *Upgrade Project Management* in SAP Solution Manager will help you. This tool contains all upgrade activities and it transparently documents all changes you make in your SAP components.

If you have to adapt your solution to new requirements, for example, by importing support packages, implementing SAP Notes, installing add-ons, changing scenarios, processes, and individual process steps, you must perform several steps before the change can be implemented in the target system. To do this, SAP Solution Manager provides the *Change Request Procedure*. This tool enables you to perform changes within your solution at a minimal risk in terms of financials and time spent.

In addition to the aforementioned tools, SAP Solution Manager provides specific functions for the operation of a system landscape:

The *Landscape Reporting* function enables you to retrieve information on your system landscape from a central location in SAP Solution Manager anytime you like.

Another function is the integrated *Support Desk*, which facilitates efficient message processing. In the Support Desk area, SAP provides you with the Incident Management functions that are necessary for Service Support. Support Desk is an integral part of SAP Solution Manager 3.1. In particular, you can map the ITIL processes Incident, Problem, and Change Management. And with the so-called Notes, you can even build up a solution database.

During operation, SAP Solution Manager enables you to monitor your systems and processes. Instead of the traditional system monitoring that focuses on only certain system components, we speak of *Solution Monitoring*. In SAP Solution Manager, solution monitoring consists of three monitoring areas:

▶ **Business Process Monitoring/Interface Monitoring**
Here the focus lies on real-time monitoring of business processes. Business process monitoring focuses on alarms for the technical operation of a business process, such as the performance of a transaction or the monitoring of interfaces.

▶ **System Monitoring**
The focal points of system monitoring are the centralized system administration and the real-time monitoring of all system components relevant to business processes.

▶ **Service Level Management (SLM) and EarlyWatch Alert (EWA)**
Service Level Management (SLM) is used to check whether agreements and objectives that have been arranged with business partners are adhered to. You can check such agreements and objectives by using the *Service Level Reporting* function in SAP Solution Manager. Service Level Reporting serves as a basis for the control of and adherence to Service Level Agreements (SLAs). It is based on the data collection of SAP EarlyWatch Alert (SAP EWA). SAP EWA is a monitoring tool that monitors certain administrative areas of SAP components. It runs automatically once a week and informs you about already existing critical or imminent problems within your system.

Chapter 2, Section 2.2, provides you with additional information on the various tools in SAP Solution Manager.

1.3   Monitoring Concept

The best monitoring tool is useless if you don't document the requirements to centralized monitoring before the configuration and implementation of the monitoring application starts. This simply means that the implementa-

tion of a monitoring system must be prepared accurately. Therefore, you have to create a monitoring concept which, among other things, describes the following:

▶ Who is the person in charge of system monitoring
▶ Who takes responsibility for which particular area
▶ Which are the specific requirements for system monitoring
▶ Which system components will be monitored
▶ Which monitoring objects will be included in the system monitoring solution
▶ How frequently will the monitoring objects have to be monitored
▶ When will an automatic notification for exceeding a threshold value have to be sent
▶ Who the automatic notification will be sent to
▶ What are the necessary procedures in the event of an escalation
▶ Which monitoring software is to be used

Keep in mind that the creation of a monitoring concept takes time. The more detailed the description of your requirements to your centralized system monitoring solution, the easier it will be to decide which monitoring components should be included in the monitoring process. And besides, don't forget that a monitoring concept can only be the basis for all other things that follow. Once it has been implemented and you start gathering your own experience in centralized monitoring, you will be able to refine your concept constantly.

In Chapter 3, you'll find information on the elements that you should include in your monitoring concept.

1.4   Project Team

Irrespective of the scope of a project, such as the implementation of centralized system monitoring via monitoring software, you have to build a project team. In doing so, you should consider the following two options: Either you build up a project team that concentrates exclusively on the design and implementation of the centralized monitoring solution, or you build up a team that does the project work in parallel (yes, concurrently) to its everyday work.

In terms of quality, we recommend that you have a dedicated project team for the design and implementation of a centralized monitoring solution that is relieved of its daily tasks.

But, apart from quality, time is also important. A dedicated project team could finish its job in a shorter timeframe, which would result in an earlier implementation and a going-live of the centralized monitoring solution.

To conclude this section, here are some general hints that will help you build up your project team:

▶ **Identify a project leader.**
  The project leader is responsible for both the design and implementation of the monitoring concept.

▶ **Identify the project members.**
  When you select the team members, make sure that every one of them shares his or her individual knowledge about system monitoring.

1.5 Toys Inc.: Initial Situation

To clarify and underline the necessity to create a monitoring concept and an implementation procedure for a centralized system monitoring solution in SAP Solution Manager, we will use the system landscape of a fictitious company, Toys Inc., as an example.

The Company

With its headquarters in the U.S., Toys Inc. is a medium-sized business that produces plastic toys. The company has three locations worldwide: Germany, Singapore, and the U.S. In each of these locations, there are two production sites and two distribution centers. The company's peak season begins in August and ends in December. In the slow season (January through July), production takes place 12 hours on weekdays. During the peak season (August through December), production is 24/7. Both the suppliers (for example, for materials) and the customers are dispersed around the globe.

System Landscape

To support the sales, production, and distribution of its products, the company uses an SAP R/3 system, while requirements for planning and production planning are carried out with SAP's supply chain management system, SCM-APO. A warehouse management system is used to administer the warehouse stocks. For the two SAP sys-

tems, a development, testing, and production system is available.

Due to the different geographical locations and time zones of the company's subsidiaries, the production systems have to be available 24 hours 7 days a week.

Application component	Description
SAP R/3	Production system
SAP R/3	Development system
SAP R/3	Testing system
SAP SCM	Production system
SAP SCM	Development system
SAP SCM	Testing system
WAMA (Non-SAP component)	Warehouse management system

Table 1.1 Software Components of the System Landscape

IT Department

The systems are serviced from the U.S. as the entire IT is located there. The IT department is structured according to the organization chart in Figure 1.2. It consists of four main groups—the Basis team, the Help-Desk team, the Warehouse Management team (which is also responsible for the SAP components), and the SAP team. Within these teams, there is a further separation of responsibilities according to the different areas of expertise.

▶ **Basis Team**
  The Basis team maintains the systems with regard to databases and operating systems. This work involves tasks like installing and administering databases and operating systems. Some members of the basis team are responsible for the creation of data backups that might be needed for a system recovery. The hardware management includes the procurement and maintenance of new hardware while the network management has to maintain the entire networking landscape. The security management group provides protection against external influences such as an undesired external access to the systems. Both the monitoring of the individual areas and the handling of user problems within the base area (support) is ensured by the individual teams.

```
                           ┌──────────────────┐
                           │  IT Department   │
                           └──────────────────┘
```

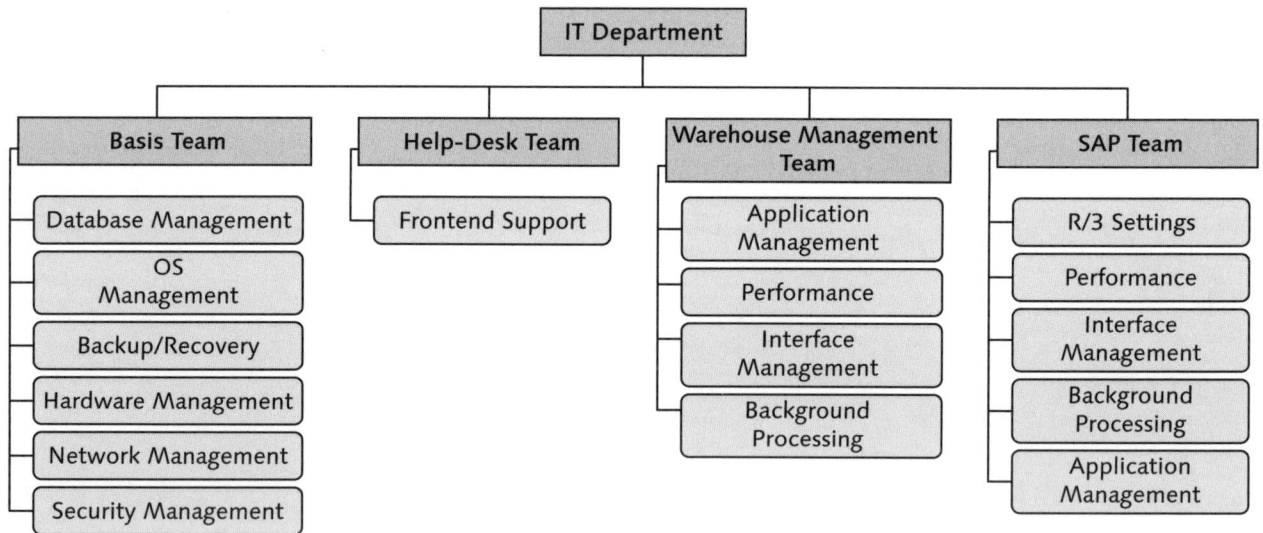

Figure 1.2 Organization Chart of the IT Department at Toys Inc.

The chart shows the IT Department with four teams:

Basis Team
- Database Management
- OS Management
- Backup/Recovery
- Hardware Management
- Network Management
- Security Management

Help-Desk Team
- Frontend Support

Warehouse Management Team
- Application Management
- Performance
- Interface Management
- Background Processing

SAP Team
- R/3 Settings
- Performance
- Interface Management
- Background Processing
- Application Management

▶ **Help-Desk Team**

The Help-Desk team maintains the front-end PCs. For example, if a user has a problem with a PC, the Help-Desk team will handle the troubleshooting.

▶ **SAP Team**

The sole goal of the SAP team is to ensure the smooth operation of SAP applications. Part of their job entails being able to foster a good system performance that involves the proper maintenance of R/3 system settings, such as the buffer settings. Interfaces like the Core Interface (CIF) between an SCM system and an R/3 system are monitored by both technical support and the application. The application management team is responsible for users and the assignment of authorizations. The most important aspect of background processing is that the systems can process all background jobs planned within a certain timeframe without reaching their resource or performance limits. The SAP team, too, performs system monitoring and provides problem solutions to the users, but only with regard to SAP applications.

▶ **Warehouse Management Team**

The fourth team in the IT department is the Warehouse Management team. Like the SAP team, it is application-oriented. The tasks of the Warehouse Management team are similar to those of the SAP team.

System Monitoring

Each member of the four teams has to perform various tasks. One of these tasks is the monitoring of the systems. When monitoring systems, every employee concentrates on that part of the system in which he or she specializes. To do this, each team member uses the tools available in their individual system areas.

Therefore, the database expert is responsible for the smooth operation of the databases in all systems. One of his or her jobs is the management of existing datasets, which means that he or she must know where to find individual datasets and check the database growth within certain periods.

An expert from the R/3 team checks the system performance on a regular basis, that is, from time to time, this expert must determine whether the response time behavior of the systems is still acceptable.

Another person monitors the resource utilization of the machines, such as the memory and CPU utilization.

From a professional point of view, this decentralized type of monitoring provides the best results in terms of quality since every one of these employees can make a reliable judgment and determine how critical or insignificant an upcoming problem might be for the running system operation. However, because all employees have the same problem, no one has an overview of the entire system landscape. There is no single point of access that handles the monitoring of all system components.

The fact that no one has a complete overview of the system landscape means that it is impossible for an individual team member to find out whether there are problems in different locations of the system that could be related to each other.

Problems with the Existing System Monitoring Process
As a result of the existing type of system monitoring and a look back into the history of the monitoring process, the following problems have emerged:

1. **Response Time – System Availability**
   One of the main problems at Toys Inc. is the long response time in terms of problem recognition, particularly with regard to system availability. It is currently not planned to use a high-availability solution. Therefore the downtime of a system can be reduced only by responding quickly to system failures. The reduction of the response time is supposed to minimize the system downtime to almost zero, especially from August through December, the necessary maintenance not being included in this calculation.

2. **SAP Buffer Settings**
   In the past, the SAP buffer settings often were the cause of performance problems. It is therefore reasonable to include the SAP buffers into the centralized system monitoring process.

3. **Job Monitoring**
   Another problem is the monitoring of background jobs that have to run regularly for technical reasons. These are maintenance jobs that are regularly planned, because they are necessary to achieve a smooth system operation. One of these jobs, for example, is the SAPConnect sending job that typically runs every 10 minutes and checks whether there is new email in the queue and if so, sends it directly from the queue. If this job doesn't run, no email can be sent from an SAP system.

4. **Database Accesses – Database Time**
   The SAP system landscape at Toys Inc. contains many proprietary developments. Previously, access paths in the proprietary applications also existed. This, in turn, led to longer database response times and subsequently to performance bottlenecks. In the future,

we must place more importance on shorter database response times in order to avoid these kinds of problems.

Overcoming the System Monitoring Problems
In order to reduce their problems with system monitoring or even avoid them altogether, Toys Inc. has decided to set up a project team. In this new project team, each team of the IT department is represented by one of its members.

The project team's objective will be to optimize the monitoring of system components within the existing solution by carrying out structural changes in the IT department and implementing a monitoring tool.

On the basis of this objective, the team has to perform the following necessary activities:

▶ Establish requirements for future system monitoring activities
▶ Establish measures to eliminate existing system monitoring problems to meet future requirements
▶ Perform these measures within a given timeframe

Because this book focuses on the design and implementation of system monitoring in the SAP Solution Manager, we will not go into more detail about the project work itself and the additional activities needed for its successful completion.

2 SAP Solution Manager

SAP Solution Manager collects information about the applications contained in a system solution and the business processes run by these applications. It therefore provides a central, transparent data source that can serve as a basis for numerous decisions and activities in your IT organization. In addition, the central data collection ensures the consistency of individual decisions and related activities.

Apart from the pure description of your solution landscape, SAP Solution Manager provides additional functions to implement and operate your SAP solution. I will briefly introduce these functions to you in the following sections.

2.1 Implementation Platform

The integration of new SAP scenarios—such as SAP Supply Chain Management (SAP SCM), SAP Supplier Relationship Management (SAP SRM), or the very first implementation of an SAP product in a system landscape—are carried out in the form of a project. Projects are process-oriented; that is, they don't focus on the implementation of just one component, but rather on the complete implementation of entire business processes so that cross-system processes are optimally supported as well. In this respect, you use the tools and utilities that are commonly used in project management.

An important project-management tool is the use of separate project phases and their sub-processes. Thus, in terms of its progress, a typical project for the implementation of an SAP solution can look like this:

1. Project preparation
2. Business blueprint
3. Realization
4. Final preparation
5. Go-live and support

SAP Solution Manager enables you to centrally manage and run the entire project from the implementation phase through to going live. Various tools and methods are available for this, and you can map all the relevant components of a project in SAP Solution Manager (see Figure 2.1).

In SAP Solution Manager, we differentiate between three different types of projects:

▶ **Implementation project**
The implementation project (see Figure 2.1) is based on the selection of business processes. There are two options for performing an implementation project. Either you set up a process structure according to one or more already existing templates, or you create your own process structure.

▶ **Template project**
The template project is used to create templates for other projects. The project structure of a template project can be used for any other project.

▶ **Upgrade project**
The upgrade project enables you to identify and perform the necessary tasks in order to upgrade an SAP component.

2.2 Solution Monitoring

When you monitor a system landscape, the most important objective is to guarantee the smooth operation of all your systems. This means you must ensure the availability and good performance of the systems. In this context, certain components of the systems or of the system landscape are checked at different planned intervals and used as a kind of "warning signal."

You can perform both automated and manual monitoring of the system landscape at the same time. In any case, you have to define Key Performance Indicators (KPIs) that serve as a basis for monitoring. Not only does

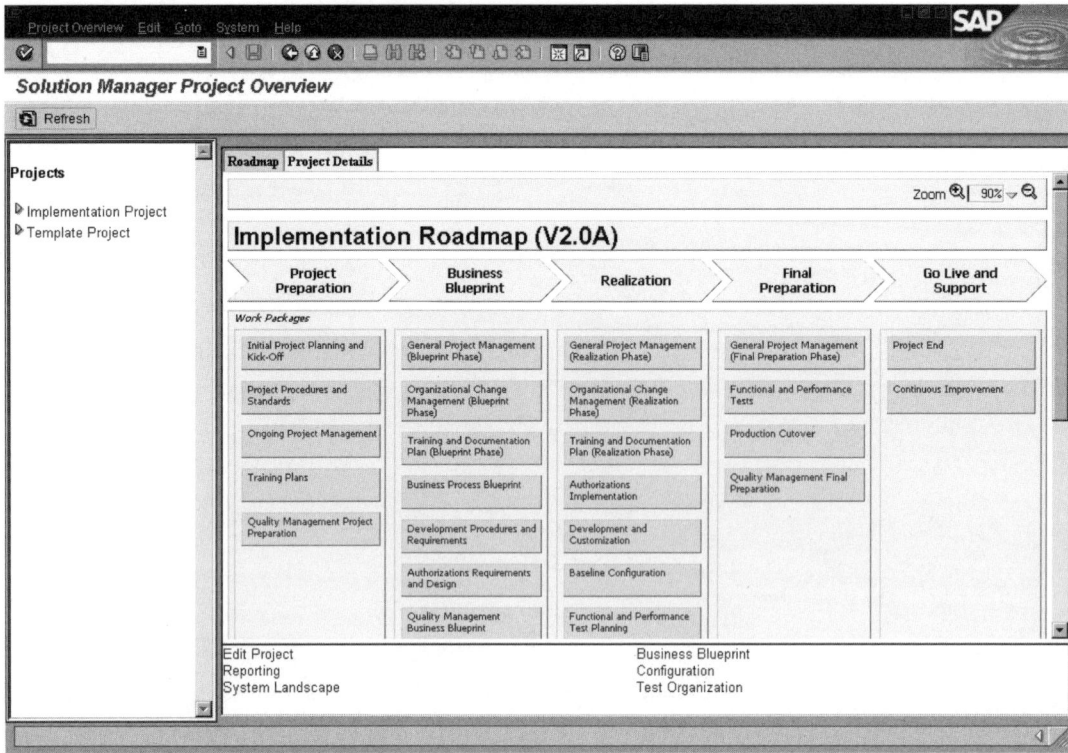

Figure 2.1   Global Project Overview in SAP Solution Manager 3.1

the term KPI imply that the systems are rated on their performance; there are many technical indicators that point to defined situations or changes of system states. In this book, I will use the term KPI for all indicators, even though not all of them are performance indicators.

Correspondingly, we will have to specify threshold values for the KPIs. The threshold values will be defined in such a way that they trigger an alarm upon the detection of a problem. The alarm either indicates that a problem will soon occur within the system landscape (proactive monitoring), or that the system is already in danger and that action must be taken immediately (reactive monitoring).

System Monitoring

In its broadest sense, the term system monitoring means the monitoring of technical components that also involves the performance and availability of a system. For example, this includes the utilization of hardware resources, databases, system availability, system configuration, R/3 configuration, OS parameters, SAP liveCache,

SAP BC, SAP IPC, SAP ITS, and so on. The administrative section of the IT department is responsible for system monitoring.

Figure 2.2 gives you an overview of the system groups in SAP Solution Manager 3.1. It displays two SAP systems with their SAP Advanced Planning and Optimization (SAP APO) and SAP R/3 components.

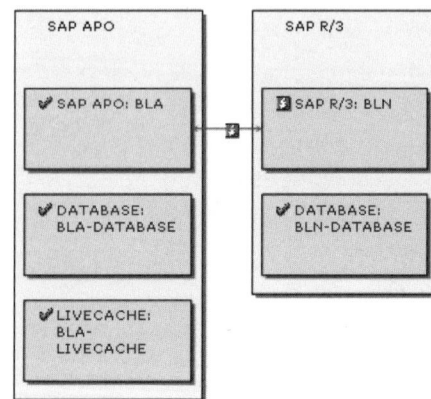

Figure 2.2   System Monitoring in SAP Solution Manager 3.1: Overview of System Groups

Business Process Monitoring

Monitoring critical business processes within a company involves business-process monitoring in an application. The main focus of this activity is the monitoring of business processes or of individual process steps that can become critical for a company if these processes fail to work properly. For example, you can monitor background processing activities within a business process. Additionally, SAP Solution Manager enables you to monitor the application logs of specific objects, such as the ALE log.

In the following example, I'll show the relationship between technical monitoring and business-process monitoring.

Demand planning, for example, is a business process, as shown in Figure 2.3. Now the question is: "To what extent does demand planning affect the database?" An I/O load is generated, which means that a specific table gets updated. How can you measure this process? Demand planning can't really be measured, but you can specify various measurement criteria, for example, the number of updates. This means that, from a technical point of view, business processes are represented as data movements, CPU load, memory load, and so on. By measuring these technical details, you can draw your own conclusions regarding the business process. Therefore, monitoring a business process is really checking its technical ramifications.

Interface Monitoring

Interface monitoring distinguishes between technical and application-oriented monitoring. Technical monitoring involves the monitoring of the entire network and the individual communication links within the system landscape. Application-oriented monitoring, on the other hand, focuses on the correct processing of jobs in the target system.

SAP Solution Manager enables you to monitor interfaces such as transactional Remote Function Call (tRFC), queued Remote Function Call (qRFC), Application Link Enabling (ALE), or Electronic Data Interchange (EDI) both from a technical- and an application-oriented viewpoint.

If you want to perform application-oriented interface monitoring, you should first map your business processes in the business-process monitoring tool of SAP Solution Manager; otherwise, it wouldn't make sense (see Figure 2.3). What does this mean?

1. You create a business process that substantially adds to the success of the company. This business process is divided into business process steps. Each of these individual business process steps performs a task in a specific component environment. If the tasks are distributed across several systems, interfaces between these systems will emerge as a result. These specific interfaces have to be monitored. Figure 2.3 illustrates an interface between two business process steps— release of final forecast (12) and transfer of data from APO into R/3 (13).

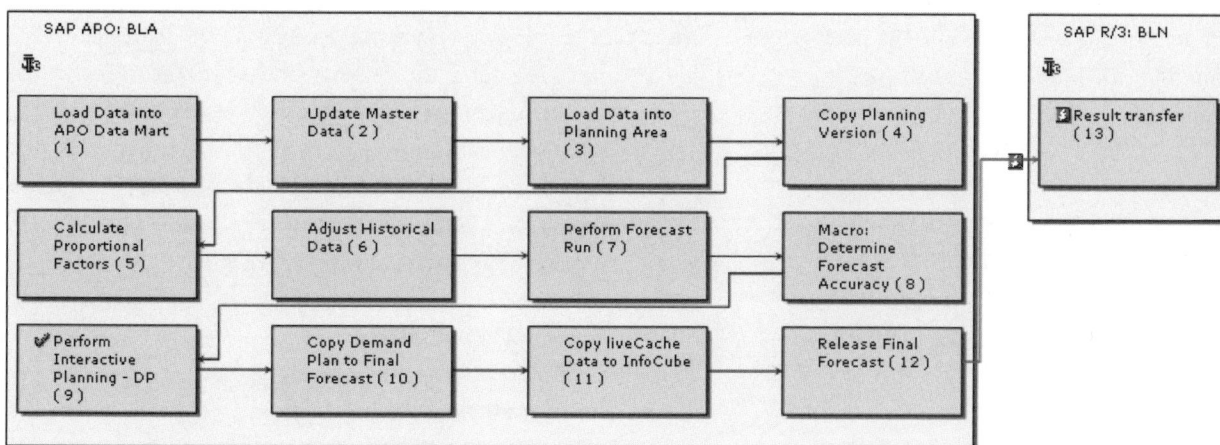

Figure 2.3 Example of Business Process Monitoring in SAP Solution Manager 3.1: Demand Planning

2. Once the business process including its individual steps has been mapped in SAP Solution Manager, you can begin to configure and set up the interface monitoring.

Figure 2.4 illustrates an application-oriented interface monitoring between two business process steps. If you double-click on the check mark (a symbol for the interface), you can obtain detailed information about the interface. You can directly assume monitoring responsibility via the application.

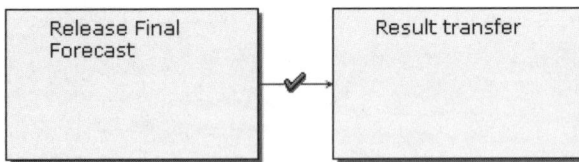

```
┌──────────────────┐          ┌──────────────────┐
│ Release Final    │          │ Result transfer  │
│ Forecast         │     ✔──▶ │                  │
│                  │          │                  │
└──────────────────┘          └──────────────────┘
```

Figure 2.4 Business-Process-Oriented Interface Monitoring in SAP Solution Manager 3.1

Figure 2.5 shows an example of technical interface monitoring. As already mentioned above, technical interface monitoring involves the monitoring of network components and individual communication links within the system landscape. In order to set up technical system monitoring, you must first map your system landscape in SAP Solution Manager. However, in contrast to application-oriented interface monitoring, you don't need to map the business processes.

Figure 2.5 illustrates two SAP systems that are linked by an interface. This interface will be included in the system-monitoring process. You can obtain detailed information about it by double-clicking on the check mark (a symbol for the interface).

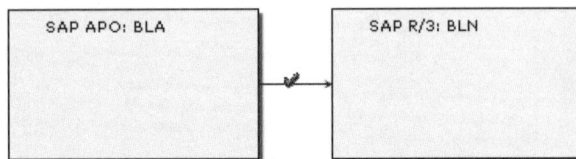

```
┌──────────────────┐          ┌──────────────────┐
│ SAP APO: BLA     │          │ SAP R/3: BLN     │
│                  │    ✔──▶  │                  │
│                  │          │                  │
└──────────────────┘          └──────────────────┘
```

Figure 2.5 Technical Interface Monitoring Between Two SAP Systems in SAP Solution Manager 3.1

Service Level Management

You do Service Level Management (SLM) in order to confirm whether agreements and objectives, which have been arranged for with a business partner, are adhered to. A business partner could be a hardware supplier, a software supplier, the implementation partner, the outsourcing partner, a customer, or a support organization.

The parties involved define requirements in the form of specific indicators (KPIs) such as system availability times or the response time behavior of certain transactions. The identification and definition of such indicators are stipulated in so-called Service Level Agreements (SLAs). Service Level Reporting, in turn, generates the results and evaluations of the SLAs.

The goal of SLM is to achieve a quality assurance that, in the long run, due to improved communication, raises the level of satisfaction for the IT organization and the users. This goal can be achieved by clearly defined objectives, instructions, budgets, and communication structures (that is, the means of communication employed between Application and Technical Groups within the IT System landscape).

Service Level Reporting

In the context of SLM, SAP Solution Manager also supports Service Level Reporting (see Figure 2.6).

Here you define the scope of reporting according to the relevant SLAs. When doing this, you can include factors from the business processes as well as indicators (for example, internal monitoring objects used by the IT team) from the system landscape. However, it is important that you know upfront which systems you want to integrate into the reporting process, what kind of information you need regarding the systems, and what type of report you prefer. Therefore, it is advisable to focus on a specific target audience. You may need either a summarized report for your managers or a rather detailed list of everything. In any case, with SAP Solution Manager, you can define and simultaneously run various different reports.

SAP EarlyWatch Alert

In addition to the Service Level Reporting functions, you have another source of documentation to create reports—the EarlyWatch Alert Service, which is automatically created once a week.

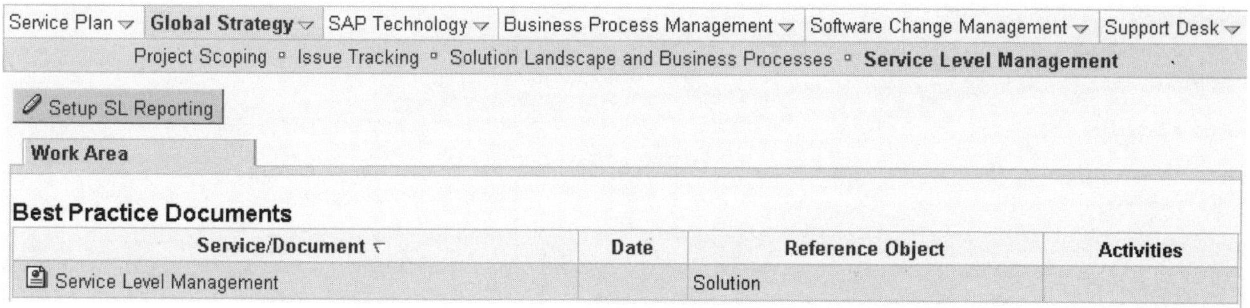

Figure 2.6 Configuration of Service Level Management in SAP Solution Manager 3.1

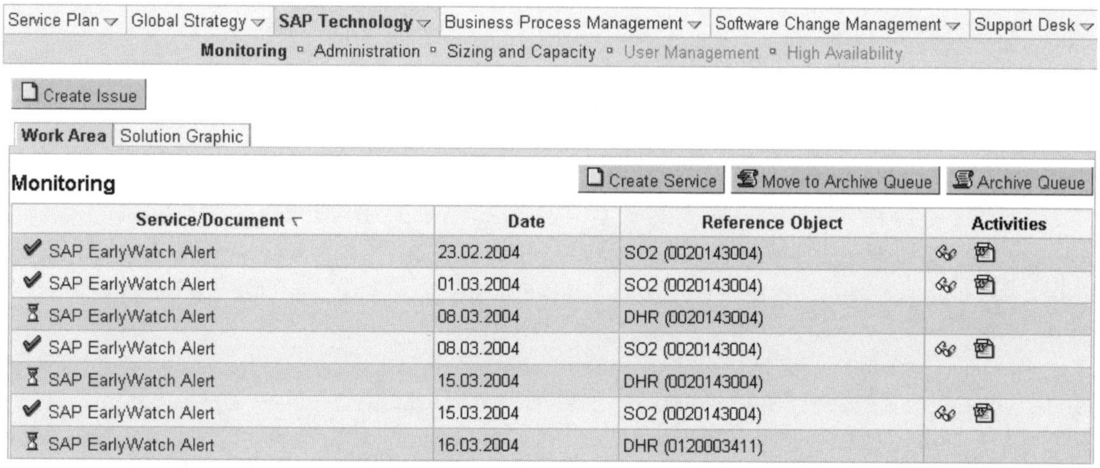

Figure 2.7 SAP EarlyWatch Alert in SAP Solution Manager 3.1

The EarlyWatch Alert provides information about the state of individual systems and their components within your system landscape.

The main difference between the Service Level Reporting functions and the EarlyWatch Alert (EWA) is that within SAP Solution Manager the former can be customized according to the specific needs of any given user. The EWA, on the other hand, doesn't need to be specifically configured. Depending on the SAP solution you use (SCM, R/3, CRM, and so on), it contains predefined default parameters such as ABAP Dump Statistics or statistics about transactions with the best response time behavior.

An EWA report is created for every SAP system you use. In Service Level Reporting, the reports contain a list of all systems along with the relevant indicators you had previously defined.

Figure 2.7 provides an overview of the EWA in SAP Solution Manager.

2.3 SAP Service Provision

To ensure a stable and high-performing system landscape, SAP provides various services that are included in SAP Safeguarding and SAP Solution Management Optimization. In the past, services were ordered either via a message in the SAPNet R/3 Frontend, or directly from an SAP contact person.

Today, SAP Solution Manager enables you to order and obtain these services as it provides a dedicated platform for doingt so. Figure 2.8 contains a list of the available services. By selecting a service, you go to the SAP Service Catalog, which provides you with a description of the individual services and information about the costs. You can also activate the ordering process from the SAP Service Catalog.

Basically, we have to distinguish between remote services, on-site services, and self-services.

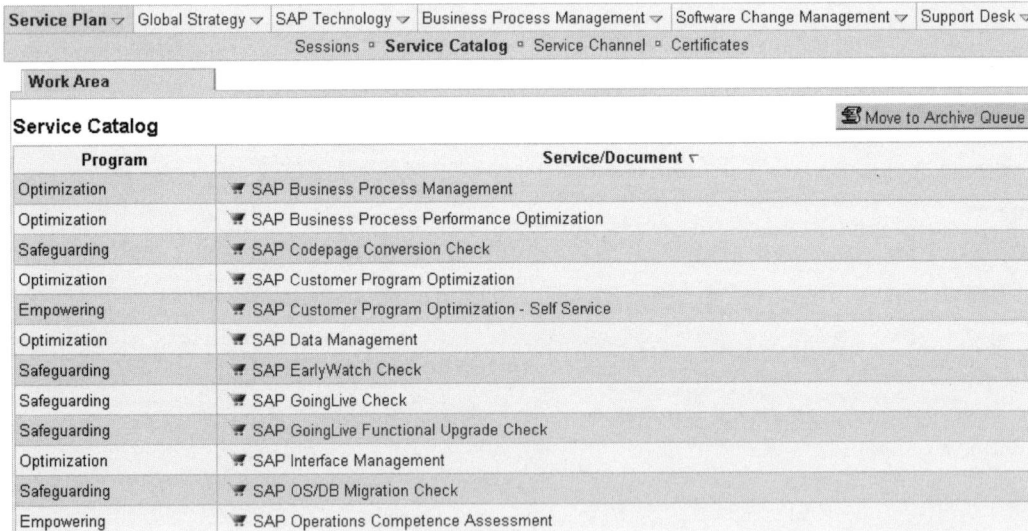

| Service Plan ▽ | Global Strategy ▽ | SAP Technology ▽ | Business Process Management ▽ | Software Change Management ▽ | Support Desk ▽ |

Sessions ▫ **Service Catalog** ▫ Service Channel ▫ Certificates

Work Area

Service Catalog   🕮 Move to Archive Queue

Program	Service/Document ▽
Optimization	☝ SAP Business Process Management
Optimization	☝ SAP Business Process Performance Optimization
Safeguarding	☝ SAP Codepage Conversion Check
Optimization	☝ SAP Customer Program Optimization
Empowering	☝ SAP Customer Program Optimization - Self Service
Optimization	☝ SAP Data Management
Safeguarding	☝ SAP EarlyWatch Check
Safeguarding	☝ SAP GoingLive Check
Safeguarding	☝ SAP GoingLive Functional Upgrade Check
Optimization	☝ SAP Interface Management
Safeguarding	☝ SAP OS/DB Migration Check
Empowering	☝ SAP Operations Competence Assessment

Figure 2.8   Service Catalog in SAP Solution Manager 3.1

Remote Services

Remote services are, for example, the SAP EarlyWatch Check, the SAP GoingLive Check, or the SAP OS/DB Migration Check. These are system services within the SAP system landscape in which an experienced SAP consultant dials into your system from a remote location and examines the system as it appears according to the requirements of the services you have purchased.

If you use SAP Solution Manager, the services are performed here. Therefore, in addition to viewing the final report on the services performed, SAP Solution Manager also enables you to view the corresponding individual tasks that were carried out during the service. This ensures a greater transparency of the service provided. If, in the future, you need the final report again, you can download it from SAP Solution Manager at any time.

On-Site Services

On-site services such as the SAP Customer Program Optimization service are performed on your site by an SAP consultant. Here, the analysis includes a specific part of the system landscape. The example described above focuses on analyzing and optimizing proprietary applications developed by the customer.

As is the case with remote services, the SAP consultant stores the results and suggested solutions in SAP Solution Manager.

For each service provided, you can generate a report that is available in SAP Solution Manager at any time.

Self-Services

Like the SAP Customer Program Optimization Self-Service, self-services aren't provided by an SAP consultant, but by an SAP customer or an SAP certified partner. As a prerequisite, the employee doing the monitoring has to be trained by SAP. In this case, that is, when the customer requests self-services, he or she is responsible for the accuracy of the analysis and the subsequent conclusions. Self-services is independent from the monitoring. The customer can decide to do a self-service as a prerequisite or after a problem arises during monitoring and IT does the service as a result.

Self-services can only be performed in SAP Solution Manager.

2.4   Service Channel: SAP Service Marketplace

There's a link between SAP Solution Manager and SAP Service Marketplace. SAP Solution Manager enables you to easily contact SAP directly via this Service Channel.

Figure 2.9 illustrates how you enter the Service Channel to SAP Service Marketplace from SAP Solution Manager. The SAP Service Channel is divided into the following folders, each of which has different functions:

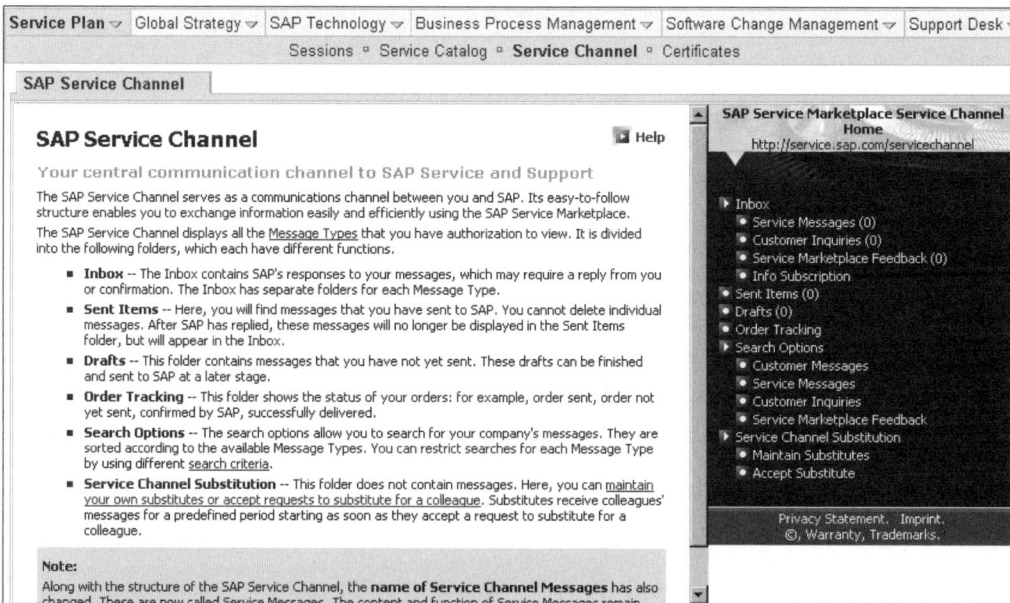

Figure 2.9 Service Channel in SAP Solution Manager 3.1

▶ **Inbox**

The *Inbox* folder contains SAP's responses to messages, which may require a reply from you or a confirmation. It has separate folders for each message type. The different message types are customer messages, business-one messages, development requests, service messages, customer enquiries, SAP Service Marketplace feedback, and purchase orders.

▶ **Sent Items**

In the *Sent Items* folder, you'll find messages that you sent to SAP. After SAP has replied, these messages will no longer be displayed in the *Sent Items* folder, but will appear in the *Inbox*.

▶ **Drafts**

This folder contains messages that you have not yet sent to SAP.

▶ **Order Tracking**

This folder shows the status of your orders (for example, order sent, order not yet sent, confirmed by SAP, and service delivered).

▶ **Search Options**

The *Search Options* folder allows you to search for your company's messages.

▶ **Service Channel Substitution**

This folder does not contain messages. Here, you can maintain your own substitutes (that is, the person to

whom you give authorization to read and process your messages when you're not in the office) or accept requests to substitute for a colleague. Substitutes receive colleagues' messages for a predefined period starting as soon as they accept a request to substitute for a colleague.

2.5 Best Practices for Solution Management

Another functionality within SAP Solution Manager is the provision of Best Practices for Solution Management. Best Practices are documents created by SAP consultants. The consultants base the contents of these documents on the experience of a multitude of customer projects in which they have been involved. The documents are updated on a regular basis.

Best Practices are divided into the following categories:

▶ System Management

▶ SAP Solution Management

▶ Application & Integration Management

▶ Software & Upgrade Management

Depending on the SAP components you use—such as CRM, SRM, and APO—SAP Solution Manager automati-

Service/Document ▽	Date	Reference Object	Activities
📄 Availability Monitoring for e-Business		Solution	
📄 Central System Monitoring for mySAP.com		Solution	
📄 Enterprise Portal System Landscape Monitoring		Solution	
📄 mySAP Enterprise Portal Volume Testing		Solution	
📄 mySAP SCM Monitoring with SAP Solution Manager and CCMS		Solution	
📄 mySAP SRM System Landscape Monitoring		Solution	

Figure 2.10   Best Practices in SAP Solution Manager 3.1

cally offers you the relevant Best Practices documents. If you use an APO system that you have linked to SAP Solution Manager, all those Best Practices documents that SAP provides for this component will be displayed.

Thus you can easily access and download these documents. This way, long searches are avoided and you get a complete overview of all the documents provided by SAP for your specific SAP components. Figure 2.10 shows a list of Best Practices documents for monitoring in the SAP Technology area.

If you want to obtain a comprehensive overview of all the Best Practices documents available, you can find them in SAP Service Marketplace at *http://service.sap.com*, quick link */solutionmanagerbp*.

2.6   IT Infrastructure Library (ITIL)

Future releases of SAP Solution Manager will see a further alignment of terminology and functionalities with the Information Technology Infrastructure Library (ITIL) standards. ITIL provides a de-facto standard for processes in IT service management. In the service management processes of the current release of SAP Solution Manager, these standards are already partly used but they still carry SAP-specific names. Figure 2.11 shows the relationships between SAP functionalities and ITIL processes. In the following sections, we will employ the commonly used SAP terminology and would like those readers who are interested in ITIL to use Figure 2.11 as a reference.

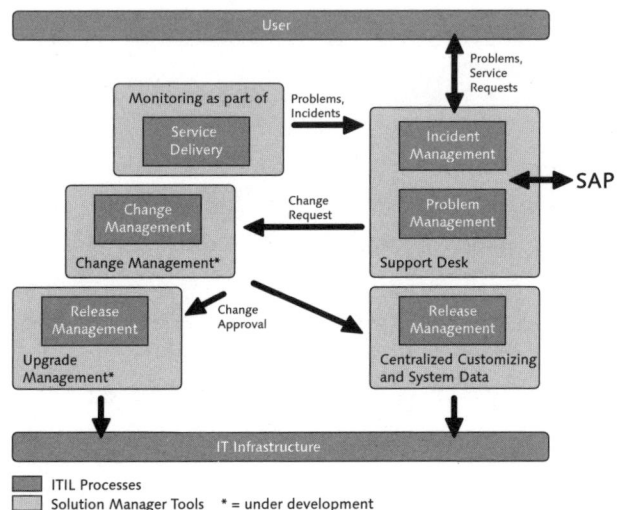

Figure 2.11   Relationship Between ITIL Processes and SAP

2.7   Support Desk

Another tool in SAP Solution Manager is the Support Desk. You use the Support Desk to centrally collect and administer all problem enquiries that arise in the applications, or during the technical operation of the various systems in your system landscape. Therefore, you have a complete overview of all messages. Due to the centralized nature of the Support Desk, you can see, among other things:

▸ What type of message has arrived
▸ What status it has
▸ Since when it has had its current status
▸ Which message has been processed

▸ Which message has been completed

▸ Whether the response time regarding the level of priority for processing this message has been observed

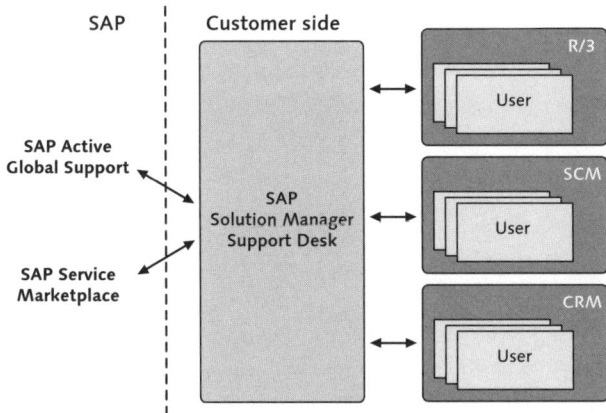

Figure 2.12 Centralized Support with SAP Support Desk

Figure 2.12 illustrates the centralized message-processing in SAP Solution Manager. Your SAP Solution Manager is connected to all your system components. Messages can be sent to SAP Solution Manager from each system component and, in turn, you can receive information about the processing status of a message. If necessary, you can forward the message to SAP for further processing. Messages to which SAP has replied are returned to customer status within SAP Solution Manager.

In the Support Desk, you can map your own support organization. You can either implement and set up your support organization in the Support Desk yourself, or do this in cooperation with an SAP consultant. But first, you must know the organizational structure of the support (that is, the definitions of functions, roles, responsibilities, and service components), the support processes, and the service level agreements.

A standard support process could look as follows:

Initial Situation: The user can no longer work in the SAP system and needs support.

Solution: She opens a message in the SAP system that she is currently using. In the **Help · Enter Support Message** menu, she can then create the message. She chooses the relevant component, enters a short text, and specifies a priority for the message after which he or she has to describe the problem. Additionally, she can also send an attachment with the message, for example, information on an ABAP dump.

When all information has been entered, the user can send the message. In this context, it means that she sends the message to the Support Desk in SAP Solution Manager. In addition to the information entered by the user, the message also contains information about the system, for example, the OS and database versions, the support-package level, and even the transaction in which the user is currently working. Thus the person who processes the message doesn't have to search for this information in the system; neither does she need to obtain information about the sender from a different location. The amount of additional information greatly facilitates the processing of the message.

In the SAP Support Desk, you can automatically assign the message to the corresponding unit within the support organization and also, to a specific person who should deal with it.

After receiving the message, the support agent has two options. He can provide a solution after receiving answers to possible questions from the sender, or, he can use the Solution Search in the solution database of the Support Desk and the integrated search for SAP Notes in SAP Service Marketplace to find a solution. In addition, the support agent can forward the message to another agent in the same support organization, or directly to SAP Active Global Support. To forward messages to SAP, an interface to the SAPNet R/3 Frontend is available.

After forwarding the message to SAP, the SAP Active Global Support will provide a solution to the problem. Every time the status of the message changes, an automatic transfer occurs. In the SAP Solution Manager system, you can specify how often the transfer has to occur.

2.8 SAP Solution Manager as a Monitoring Tool

Toys Inc. has decided to use SAP Solution Manager 3.1 for its centralized system monitoring. It is the company's top priority to ensure that the systems run 24 hours a day with a high performance according to the system availability requirements.

Why did the management at Toys Inc. decide to use SAP Solution Manager? One important reason is that SAP Solution Manager can be used for both proactive and reactive system monitoring.

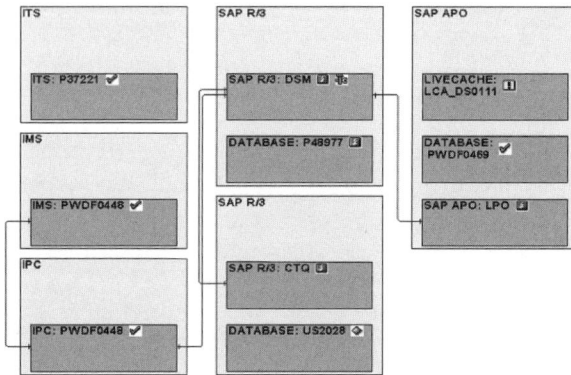

Figure 2.13   Example: Illustration of System Monitoring in SAP Solution Manager

▶ **Proactive system monitoring**

Before you can do proactive system monitoring, you must learn which monitoring objects can become indicators of a possible critical system situation. The critical situation can be avoided if the responsible team takes early action against it. As shown in Figure 2.13, SAP Solution Manager provides you with a corresponding graphic. This graphic displays the overall status of the systems and their components, and it enables you to request detailed information about individual monitoring objects.

▶ **Reactive monitoring**

The term reactive means that corrective action is taken only after a critical event has occurred. To do this, you need indicators that can alert you of the occurrence of such events. As the central monitoring system, SAP Solution Manager provides the functionality you need to send messages from a central location to the relevant person in charge. This simply means that if in a specific system an alarm— which is linked to an automatic message—is triggered, this message is sent immediately from SAP Solution Manager. Such a message can be an email or a Short Message Service (SMS).

▶ **Automated monitoring**

Automated system monitoring is done via the Alert Monitor. The Alert Monitor is part of the Computing Center Management System (CCMS). It supports the monitoring and operation of individual components in a system landscape. SAP Solution Manager refers to the monitoring architecture of the CCMS. From here, it retrieves information about specific monitoring objects. In order to perform automated monitoring, you must first define monitoring attributes and their threshold values.

▶ **Manual monitoring**

For manual system monitoring, you must have profound professional expertise. This is why only administrators and other experts perform this kind of monitoring; they often have experience in various areas of system monitoring and systems analysis. Not only can they identify critical system states, but they are also well equipped to recommend solutions that help avoid such problems.

Manual system monitoring is done in dedicated monitoring screens. For example, in an SAP environment you can use Transaction ST03N to call the Workload Monitor. Here, statistical data about response times, memory usage, and database accesses is collected and stored for each transaction. This data is then summarized and can be used to examine the load distribution within an R/3 system.

3 Designing the Monitoring Concepts

Before you can implement an efficient monitoring system, you must first define the monitoring criteria and procedures. These factors are summarized in a monitoring concept that is the basis for the implementation process.

This chapter provides you with basic information for designing a monitoring concept and, on the basis of the system landscape at Toys Inc., lists several necessary monitoring objects as integral parts of this concept. The list consists of a specific selection of monitoring objects, which you can use as a foundation for your own concept. Note that this chapter does not provide you with a comprehensive monitoring concept, as various kinds of system information can play an important role in monitoring. This heterogeneous information is because of the different requirements of system operations and the use of additional SAP and non-SAP components that aren't addressed in this book.

Instead, this chapter is designed for those readers who are interested in learning general information about monitoring concepts, as well as system administrators who are responsible for system monitoring.

3.1 The Monitoring Concept

The monitoring concept is the initial system monitoring document. It details the specific system monitoring requirements, the organization of personnel, and the way in which various processes flow within system monitoring work, for example, troubleshooting or escalation procedures.

You continuously have to tailor the document so it reflects new developments and changes in the overall process. You should use this document as a guide for outlining responsibilities, and drafting rules for specific activities, escalation procedures, and the like. Therefore, you should appoint a responsible person to deal with change requests and innovations regarding system monitoring. This person alone should make the changes to the monitoring concept after seriously considering if these changes are necessary.

Although this may not appear to be a particularly important aspect of system monitoring for some, you should ensure that the system monitoring document can be accessed by all those involved. Both contact persons (for example, the database expert who will be involved after a database problem has been recognized during the monitoring process, or the manager who will be contacted when a problem occurs that cannot be resolved in a fixed timeframe) and those who are directly involved in system monitoring should be able to access it from a central location. Suppose an escalation process needs to be started. The person responsible for jumpstarting this process has just joined the company, and there's no one available to provide information about the process. In such cases, what options would be available so you could react within a specified timeframe? The answer is easy: Follow the instructions in the system monitoring document.

The following sections describe the components that can be part of a monitoring concept. They're intended to be mere suggestions and pointers for you if you have to develop a monitoring concept for your own system landscape that will meet the requirements of both you and your users.

Requirements of System Monitoring

The first part of the monitoring concept should describe the general requirements of system monitoring. This part should not contain any other details such as the specification of monitoring objects and their threshold values; rather, it should consider those issues that regularly caused problems in the past and that might affect a smooth system operation in the future. We recommend that the project group clarify these issues in their first meeting. Towards the end of the concept design phase, you should ensure that the list of requirements has been included in its entirety in the concept.

Documenting the System Landscape

When designing the monitoring concept, it is important that you get a complete overview of the system landscape. The overview should contain a presentation of the landscape structure that includes all systems in use, or only those systems that are required for a productive system operation. The systems to be included in the structural overview differ in each individual landscape. However, I strongly recommend that you include all your systems. Therefore, upon completion of the monitoring concept, your documentation will be comprehensive. And please don't forget that this documentation will later serve as the basis for setting up the system landscape in SAP Solution Manager. The more details you consider, the less time you'll need for additional information gathering during the set-up phase.

For the purpose of clarification, we advise you to divide the system landscape into several areas according to the application components used, as described in Table 3.1. Here, the SAP application components are considered with regard to our sample company, Toys Inc.

SAP application component	Product release	SID	Installation number	System description
SAP R/3	6.20	BLN	0020096422	Production system
SAP R/3	6.20	BEN	0020096423	Development system
SAP R/3	6.20	BTN	0020096424	Testing system
SAP SCM	4.0	BLA	0120003412	Production system
SAP SCM	4.0	BEA	0120003413	Development system
SAP SCM	4.0	BTA	0120003414	Testing system

Table 3.1 SAP System Landscape at Toys Inc.

Depending on the solution implemented, an SAP application can contain additional technical components apart from the central database. For example, in the SAP SCM

solution you can use APO, the Inventory Collaboration Hub (ICH), or the Event Manager (EM).

If you use APO, as we do in our example with Toys Inc., you need liveCache—a technical component that runs on the same host as the APO solution. Of course, you can also use liveCache on a different host, that is, as distinct from your APO solution. Alternatively, you can also use optimizers with your APO solution; however, this depends on the type of applications that you use within the APO solution. Table 3.2 summarizes these technical components.

SID	Component	Server	Release	Name
BLA	liveCache	PWDF0445	7.4.2.20	LCA
BEA	liveCache	PWDF0446	7.4.2.20	LCE
BTA	liveCache	PWDF0447	7.4.2.20	LCT

Table 3.2 Additional APO Components of the System Landscape at Toys Inc.

A third overview should contain hardware information for the SAP systems. The information should include the server names, the hardware vendor, the server model, the number of CPUs, the size of the main memory, and the operating system including its version number.

Table 3.3 contains an overview of the hardware configuration at Toys Inc. Each SAP system runs on a separate machine.

Another important aspect is the description of the database systems in use, including their version numbers. You should also create an overview for this information.

Table 3.4 shows that Toys Inc. uses the SAP DB database system for all its systems. The databases of the individual systems run on the same machine as the applications used.

Non-SAP as well as SAP systems are part of the overall solution. Thus, for the non-SAP systems, the relevant information also has to be collected. Table 3.5 shows the Warehouse Management Solution at Toys Inc. for which the product WAMA is used.

Table 3.6 contains an overview of the hardware configuration on the basis of which the WAMA solution has been implemented.

SID of the solution	Instance	Server name	Hardware vendor	Server model	CPU frequency (MHz)	Number of CPUs	Memory (GB)	Operating system, version
BLN	Ls8000_BLN_00	ls8000	ABC Enterprises	Premium 800	800	5	10	Basis 3.0
BEN	Ls8001_BEN_00	ls8001	ABC Enterprises	Premium 800	800	5	10	Basis 3.0
BTN	Ls8002_BTN_00	ls8002	ABC Enterprises	Premium 800	800	5	10	Basis 3.0
BLA	PWDF0445_BLA_00	PWDF0445	ABC Enterprises	Premium 900	900	8	25	Basis 3.0
BEA	PWDF0446_BEA_00	PWDF0446	ABC Enterprises	Premium 900	900	8	25	Basis 3.0
BTA	PWDF0447_BTA_00	PWDF0447	ABC Enterprises	Premium 900	900	8	25	Basis 3.0

SID	Database server	Database system, version
BLN	ls8000	SAP DB 7.3.0
BEN	ls8001	SAP DB 7.3.0
BTN	ls8002	SAP DB 7.3.0
BLA	PWDF0445	SAP DB 7.3.0
BEA	PWDF0446	SAP DB 7.3.0
BTA	PWDF0447	SAP DB 7.3.0

Table 3.4 Database Overview of the SAP System Landscape at Toys Inc.

SID	Product/ Version	Producer	Server name	Description
WAMA	WAMA 01	Outside Inc.	PDFA040	Warehouse management system

Table 3.5 Overview of Non-SAP Systems as Part of the Overall Solution at Toys Inc.

SID of the solution	WAMA
Server name	WAMA99
Hardware vendor	ABC Enterprises
Server model	Premium 800
CPU frequency (MHz)	800
Number of CPUs	5
Memory (GB)	10
Operating system, version	Basis 3.0

Table 3.6 Hardware Overview of Non-SAP Systems in the Overall Solution at Toys Inc.

Defining Roles and Responsibilities

If centralized system monitoring exists, you must appoint a person with sole responsibility to oversee this system. If possible, this person should also maintain the monitoring concept and act as the single point of contact for system monitoring.

In addition, you should create a directory with the names of the contact persons for the system monitoring group. Such a directory could look like the one used at Toys Inc., as shown in Table 3.7. As you can see, there is only one contact person for each area within the team.

Team	Contact for	Name of contact person	Phone/ Mail
Basis team	Database management system	...	...
	OS management	...	...
	Backup/Recovery	...	...
	Hardware management	...	...
	Network management	...	...
	Security management	...	...
Help-Desk team	Frontend support	...	...
Warehouse management team	Application management	...	...

Table 3.7 Directory of Contact Persons for System Monitoring Responsibilities at Toys Inc.

Team	Contact for	Name of contact person	Phone/Mail
	Performance monitoring	...	...
	Interface management	...	...
	Background processing	...	...
SAP team	R/3 settings	...	...
	Performance monitoring	...	...
	Interface management	...	...
	Background processing	...	...
	Application management	...	...

Table 3.7 Directory of Contact Persons for System Monitoring Responsibilities at Toys Inc. (cont.)

In companies that outsource the maintenance of their hardware, the responsibilities would be quite different and the list of contacts would certainly be shorter than that of our would-be company, Toys Inc.

Let's suppose that the hardware maintenance company provides a dedicated support person for each customer system. This means that the support person decides which system components will be integrated into the monitoring process and what needs to be done in an emergency situation. It also means that this person is the point of contact for both the monitoring team and the customer. Thus, in case of an emergency, it doesn't matter if the problem is related to a database, the operating system, or anything else. The administrator is always the first contact for the monitoring team and manages the entire troubleshooting process. He or she must also contact the customer if the problem leads to a prolonged system downtime that exceeds the given servicing timeframe.

Needless to say, a system consultant cannot work on a 24/7 basis. Therefore, you should organize a standby service that can be called in case of emergency.

Defining Monitoring Processes

If you want to create standards for centralized system monitoring, you must include a description of the monitoring process:

▶ **Basic conditions for the monitoring process**
For example, you have to define the number of hours necessary per day for the complete monitoring process. To a certain degree, this depends on how long the systems have to be available each day and at what times; moreover, it is important to know which effects can be expected if the monitoring of specific system components is continued the following day. Typically, in most companies there is a standby service that can be notified via Short Message Service (SMS) or pager in the event of serious problems, even in those companies that haven't implemented any continuous system monitoring.

▶ **Executing the monitoring process**
There must be clarification as to how the system monitoring process is to be executed. In this respect, you must specify what needs to be monitored and at which intervals. The person that carries out the system monitoring needs instructions as to how he or she has to respond to alarms.

▶ **Troubleshooting/Escalation process**
What happens when an alarm has been triggered? You have to react. Either the problem can be solved immediately after the alarm was triggered, or you must start an escalation procedure because the problem is severe and cannot be solved within the given timeframe. In the latter case, you need an emergency plan. You have to define which people will be involved in the escalation process and what actions need to be taken during the escalation.

Monitoring Objects

Monitoring objects are components within an IT environment such as the memory of a server or the background processing. Every monitoring object possesses specific attributes. For example, these attributes can be measurement values, statuses or messages, the memory utilization, or the average runtime of a background job.

There are many different monitoring objects within a system monitoring process. What's critical is that you identify those objects that are critical to ensure a smooth system operation of an application. As we described in Section 3.1.1, the catalog of requirements serves as the basis for the selection of monitoring objects. Furthermore, any existing agreements (service level agreements, SLAs) regarding system availability and system performance—that might have been made between the IT department and the application vendor—play an equally important role.

When you begin selecting the monitoring objects, it's quite useful to create an overview that categorizes and prioritizes the necessary monitoring objects as shown in Table 3.8. In this way, you can obtain a comprehensive view of the monitoring objects that you want to integrate into your monitoring process.

Category	Monitoring object	Priority
OS	File systems	high
	CPU	high
	Memory	high
R/3	Availability of instances	very high
Background processing	Jobs	high
ABAP dumps	R/3 ABAP	medium

Table 3.8 Categorizing and Prioritizing the Monitoring Objects

You will find more information about possible monitoring objects in Section 3.2. In this section, we'll introduce and describe some monitoring objects that can be integrated in centralized system monitoring. As we already mentioned, you must decide which objects you want to monitor.

Threshold-Value Definitions

Threshold-value definitions are an important prerequisite for automated system monitoring. They help you define the exact point at which an alarm for a monitoring attribute will be generated when the value exceeds or falls below the threshold. Threshold-value definitions are specified in different units, for example, in percentages, milliseconds, or as a quantity.

As a kind of preparation for defining and later integrating the threshold values in the SAP Solution Manager system, Table 3.9 shows the four different threshold values for a monitoring attribute that exist in the monitoring console of an SAP environment.

Theshold value	Presentation in the monitoring console
Green → Yellow	Yellow
Yellow → Red	Red
Red → Yellow	Yellow
Yellow → Green	Green

Table 3.9 Threshold Values in the SAP Monitoring Console

An attribute that currently possesses the alert color green changes its alert color to yellow when it exceeds or falls below the threshold value. The same applies to the change from yellow to red and vice versa.

If the value of an attribute constantly fluctuates above or below a certain threshold value, the alert status may constantly change. To avoid this, you can assign different threshold values for a change from green to yellow and from yellow to green. The same applies to the change from yellow to red and vice versa.

Once you have defined the monitoring objects to be included in the system monitoring process, you define the corresponding threshold values (see Table 3.10).

For example, if the file system is used at more than 90%, the alert color will change from green to yellow. If the utilization increases to 98% or higher, the alert color will change from yellow to red. If action is taken in response to the alarm and free space is created, the alert color will change back from red to yellow when the value falls below 95%. Once the threshold value of 85% has been reached, the alert color will change again from yellow to green.

Monitoring attribute	Threshold values			
	Green to yellow	Yellow to red	Red to yellow	Yellow to green
Free space requirement of file system	90%	98%	95%	85%
CPU utilization	60%	80%	75%	55%
Number of jobs canceled	5	10	9	2

Table 3.10 Threshold-Value Definition: Overview

Monitoring Frequency

The next thing you have to clarify is how often the attribute of the monitoring object has to be monitored. In this context, you must differentiate between an automated and a manual system monitoring. For automated system monitoring, only the „constantly" frequency is available. Objects that are monitored manually can be checked on a daily, weekly, monthly, or yearly basis, or as needed.

The instance availability, for example, has to be ensured on a constant basis and should therefore be included in a constant system monitoring. It's a good idea to create an overview of your monitoring attributes and the corresponding periods in which they have to be checked (see Table 3.11).

Monitoring attribute	Monitoring frequency
Instance availability	constantly
Free space requirement of file system	constantly
Average response time of dialog service	weekly
Database growth	monthly

Table 3.11 Overview of the Monitoring Frequencies for Monitoring Attributes

Alert Notification

In the event of an alarm, certain monitoring objects that have a high priority should also be equipped with a notification method. If an alarm becomes visible in the SAP Solution Manager system, an autoreaction is started simultaneously, with alerts sent either to a predefined number of people or only to the person in charge of system monitoring who, in turn, initiates all further alarm procedures according to the specified instructions.

3.2   Operating System

At the Operating-System (OS) level, there are some important components that you have to include in the system monitoring process, because the occurrence of problems may result in a chain reaction and affect the entire system landscape, which can lead to a system standstill.

The final part of each of the following sections contains an overview table that summarizes the most important characteristics of the corresponding component with regard to system monitoring.

File System

The file system consists of different files that are structured according to their function. Any problem that occurs in the file system affects the entire process flow of an application. It is therefore imperative that you include the file system in your centralized system monitoring process. One of the main reasons to do so is that you should monitor the available free hard disk space in the file system or—vice versa—the percentage of used space. A file system without any free space can lead to an application standstill as no additional information can be stored or modified within the file system.

Category	Operating system
Monitoring object	File system
Monitoring attribute of the object	Free space requirement of file system
Responsibility	Centralized system monitoring
Type of monitoring	Automated
Autoreaction method	Yes

Table 3.12   Monitoring the Use of Disk Space in the File System

CPU

Systems with a constant high utilization of CPU resources can have a negative impact on the response times and the performance of a system landscape, which is why it is important to monitor the average use of a system's CPUs.

If you detect a high CPU utilization, it doesn't necessarily mean that there is a hardware bottleneck, as the causes for this high utilization value can be manifold. Instead, you must distinguish between a continuously high utilization of the CPU resources and a temporary one. This means that when you receive an alarm for a high CPU utilization, you should watch and analyze the underlying problem. As a rule of thumb, you can say that for a period of over one hour, the free portion of CPU should have an average value of at least 20%. A value of 35% of free CPU capacity would be even more desirable. For the analysis, SAP provides different monitors such as the OS monitor (Transaction ST06) and the Workload monitor (Transaction ST03N).

Category	Operating system
Monitoring object	CPU
Monitoring attribute of the object	Average CPU utilization
Responsibility	Centralized system monitoring
Type of monitoring	Automated
Autoreaction method	No

Table 3.13 Monitoring the Average CPU Utilization

Memory Utilization — Paging

Monitoring the utilization of the main memory is just as important as monitoring the CPU utilization. Bottlenecks of the main memory can be made visible by paging. Here, we have another rule of thumb: If less than 20% of physical memory is stored in a paging file on the hard disk, you can consider the situation as being non-critical.

High paging rates occur when too many processes are run on the system or when there's insufficient memory available for running processes. In addition to monitoring the CPU utilization, you should check whether the paging process is negatively impacting the system response times and, if so, whether this is contributing to the degradation of system performance. Depending on your findings, you should then decide whether further analysis is warranted.

You will note that the different operating systems have different characteristics. A high paging rate does not always indicate that there is a memory bottleneck. It is also important to know whether a high paging rate can be detected on several different machines or on a specific one and, also, whether you are dealing with a general problem or a specific one that extensively allocates memory.

Category	Operating system
Monitoring object	Memory utilization — paging
Monitoring attribute of the object	Average memory utilization
Responsibility	Centralized system monitoring
Type of monitoring	Automated
Autoreaction method	No

Table 3.14 Monitoring the Average Memory Utilization

Swap Space

Swap space (allocated storage space) is hard disk storage space configured for storing data from the main memory. It is used when there is not enough physical memory available. If the swap space is configured too small, that is, if there are not enough memory resources available for the SAP system, the database and additional programs — this can result in memory management problems, or even a complete system failure. Therefore, you must regularly check the value of utilized swap space.

Category	Operating system
Monitoring object	Swap space
Monitoring attribute of the object	Utilization of the allocated storage space on the hard disk
Responsibility	Centralized system monitoring
Type of monitoring	Automated
Autoreaction method	No

Table 3.15 Monitoring the Use of Swap Space

Operating System Collector

The operating system collector runs on every SAP application server and database system. The SAPOSCOL program collects system data of the OS, which is then transmitted to the monitoring architecture. It is advisable to monitor the status of the operating system collector; otherwise, no operating system data is collected.

Category	Operating system
Monitoring object	Operating system collector
Monitoring attribute of the object	Status of operating system collector
Responsibility	Centralized system monitoring
Type of monitoring	Automated
Autoreaction method	Yes

Table 3.16 Monitoring the Operating System Collector Status

3.3 System and Instance Availability

Basically every company wants to keep the costs for its data centers as low as possible. On the other hand, the expectations of users and the demands to the systems are set at a high level. The systems must be available around-the-clock, which is not always possible because of limited budgets. Therefore, it is reasonable to consider the implementation of sophisticated high-availability solutions such as server mirroring or a clustering solution, especially if a 24/7 availability has to be ensured. The related costs, though, are very high.

Irrespective of whether a system has to be available for 12 or 24 hours, you should include the monitoring of the systems' availability and their application servers into the centralized monitoring process. By doing this, you ensure that the systems are available in the required timeframe and are problem-free.

Let's recall the problems that occurred previously in the system monitoring process at Toys Inc. and were recorded by the project group (see Section 1.5). A very important aspect was the response time regarding the problem identification in the case of a system availability failure in a 24/7 system operation. A system failure should not first be noted by users or other persons who don't deal with the system operation directly; rather, the system administrator should be the first to notice the problem.

In the SAP environment you can use the availability agent CCMSPING to check the availability of the message server. If the system is active, the message server will respond to the request from the availability agent. At the same time, this means that at least one application server has been registered as being active in the message server.

Category	System and instance availability
Monitoring object I	System availability
Monitoring object II	Instance availability
Monitoring attribute of the object I	Availability per system
Monitoring attribute of the object II	Status of instance availability
Responsibility	Centralized system monitoring
Type of monitoring	Automated
Autoreaction method	Yes

Table 3.17 Monitoring the System and Instance Availability

3.4 Background Processing

Although we notice an increasing tendency towards dialog-oriented processes, a large number of them still run in the background. While the IT systems have to be available for dialog and online applications during the day, both the system administrators and the application team (that is, the developers and users) schedule regular batch jobs that are run at night. Whether the background processing runs by day or night, it has to be checked regularly for errors and failures.

We distinguish between two different areas when monitoring background processes:

The first area takes a rather global view of background processing. It focuses primarily on:

▶ The average utilization of the background work processes of a server
▶ The number of errors in background work processes
▶ The program errors during the execution of background jobs
▶ The number of canceled jobs on an application server

The second area focuses on monitoring specific jobs. Here, you check the runtime behavior, whether the scheduled jobs were run correctly, whether jobs have to be rescheduled or activated manually, or whether they have to be run again and also, which jobs were canceled. For jobs that can have a substantial effect on a system's performance, we recommend that you install the automatic notification function.

Category	Background processing
Monitoring object	Background processing service—system-wide
Monitoring attribute of the object	Number of jobs ready to run and authorized to start
Responsibility	Centralized system monitoring
Type of monitoring	Automated
Autoreaction method	No

Table 3.18 Monitoring System-Wide Background Processing

Category	Background processing
Monitoring object	Background processing service—per application server
Monitoring attribute I of the object	Average utilization of background processes
Monitoring attribute II of the object	Number of errors in background work processes
Monitoring attribute III of the object	Program errors during the execution of background jobs
Monitoring attribute IV of the object	Number of jobs canceled on an application server
Responsibility	Centralized system monitoring
Type of monitoring	Automated
Autoreaction method	No

Table 3.19 Monitoring the Background Processes per Application Server

Category	Background processing
Monitoring object	Background processing—per job
Monitoring attribute I of the object	Runtime of the job
Monitoring attribute II of the object	Time delay until job starts
Monitoring attribute III of the object	Job status
Responsibility	Centralized system monitoring
Type of monitoring	Automated
Autoreaction method	Yes (depending on the importance of the job)

Table 3.20 Monitoring the Background Processes per Job

In addition to the general criteria for monitoring background processes described above, we would also like to mention the use and integration of a job scheduler into your system monitoring model. A job scheduler can also be called a background-processing control system. It automatically starts and monitors background processes.

You can integrate the job scheduler into an existing operating system; however, you should note that its control concepts are often rather basic. Therefore, we believe that platform-independent job scheduling software is a far better solution. There are a number of software producers that offer their own solutions in this area, which consist of entire job control programs or add-ons to schedulers that are already integrated in ERP products or operating systems.

When you use a job scheduler, you not only define the specific jobs themselves, but processes that enable you to restart jobs after a failure, or to respond appropriately if individual batch runs build on each other and consequently reschedule follow-up jobs. Even when a complete system failure occurs, job schedulers can reorganize the job chains because of processes you had previously defined. In other words, the jobs are interdependent.

However, despite all this automation, you cannot get along entirely without monitoring the background processes. For example, you have to manually restart batch jobs that repeatedly started automatically and were not fully completed.

With regard to centralized system monitoring, job schedulers provide only fairly limited monitoring functionalities. Because their main task is monitoring the background processes, this limited functionality shouldn't come as a surprise. Other monitoring criteria such as the system availability and buffer settings are not important to them. But if your objective is a genuine centralized system monitoring of a heterogeneous system landscape, you have to implement an interface between the central monitoring system and the job scheduler. Such an interface would enable a regular transfer of data from the job scheduler to the central monitoring system.

A good example of a job scheduling software solution is Cronacle developed by Redwood Software, which you can use to control background processes in SAP solutions. Not only does Cronacle have an interface to the CCMS so that the necessary data to control the background processes is made available, but there is also an interface to the SAP Solution Manager system that enables you to transfer the background processing results to the central monitoring system (SAP Solution Manager).

3.5 System Performance

If you continuously monitor the performance of your system, you will be able to identify and avoid problems before they occur. There are many reasons for problems with the system performance. Perhaps your hardware is not configured to handle the existing loads or the configuration of your entire system is not optimal. Possibly only some specific programs that you use are very time-intensive and use a lot of system resources so that a few tuning measures could help to improve the overall performance. On the other hand, a database performance problem could also be the cause. To find the right solutions for SAP systems, you first have to do a workload analysis. To support the workload analysis, SAP systems contain an analysis tool, the Workload Monitor (Transaction ST03N). It provides you with information about response time behaviors, throughputs, and loads in an SAP system. You should use this tool as the first step of an extensive and detailed analysis.

Possible performance problems may occur in dialog operation, background processing (see Section 3.4), and spool and update service. See Tables 3.21 to 3.24 for selected information from possible monitoring objects that are to be monitored for each application server. These monitoring objects refer to the general system performance. Using this information, you make initial conclusions and perform additional detailed analyses in the event of an emergency.

If you need further detailed information about SAP performance optimization, you should refer to the latest edition of *SAP Performance Optimization* by Thomas Schneider, also published by SAP PRESS. Regardless of which SAP solution you have to administer, Schneider's book helps you to systematically identify and analyze performance problems for any SAP solution and, also, to develop a solution approach.

For many SAP users, an important value is still the average response time of a transactional step in a dialog. On the basis of this criterion, they can evaluate the system performance. In an R/3 system, the performance is good if the average dialog response time is approximately one second. However, due to the different requirements of the systems established by various business processes and the individual configuration of a system landscape, you cannot use this rule for all R/3 systems or every SAP solution (SAP APO, SAP CRM, SAP BW, and so forth). On the contrary, every system landscape has to be regarded individually. Depending on the SAP solution you have implemented, the average dialog response time can vary considerably. As a kind of reference value, you can use the ratio between the average response time and the average database time in dialog operation mode. If the

value for the database time is more than 40% higher than that for the average response time, this could indicate a possible database or network problem, or a CPU bottleneck.

Category	System performance
Monitoring object	Dialog service
Monitoring attribute I of the object	Average response time of dialog service
Monitoring attribute II of the object	Average use of dialog work processes of an application server
Monitoring attribute III of the object	Average database time of dialog service
Monitoring attribute IV of the object	Number of dialog work processes in PRIV mode
Monitoring attribute V of the object	Wait time in the dispatcher queue
Monitoring attribute VI of the object	Time for long lasting dialog work processes
Responsibility	Centralized system monitoring
Type of monitoring	Automated
Autoreaction method	No

Table 3.21 Monitoring the Dialog Service

Category	System performance
Monitoring object	Spool service
Monitoring attribute I of the object	Average utilization of spool work processes
Monitoring attribute II of the object	Used spool numbers of SPO_NUM number range in the system
Responsibility	Centralized system monitoring
Type of monitoring	Automated
Autoreaction method	No

Table 3.22 Monitoring the Spool Service

Category	System performance
Monitoring object	Updating—system-wide
Monitoring attribute of the object	Number of wrong update requests
Responsibility	Centralized system monitoring
Type of monitoring	Automated
Autoreaction method	Yes

Table 3.23 Monitoring Updating System-Wide

Category	System performance
Monitoring object	Updating—per application server
Monitoring attribute I of the object	Wait time in the dispatcher queue
Monitoring attribute II of the object	Utilization of update work processes
Monitoring attribute III of the object	Update error in work process
Responsibility	Centralized system monitoring
Type of monitoring	Automated
Autoreaction method	No

Table 3.24 Monitoring Updating per Application Server

3.6 Traces

Traces are used to monitor the system and to isolate problems that occur in an SAP system. When you switch on a trace, various application operations are logged.

There are two types of traces: developer traces and performance traces. However, you should use the trace functions only in exceptional circumstances, because they can negatively affect system performance due to the increased write activities. Therefore, we recommend that you routinely check whether the traces are switched on and if so, whether they will impact the system operation and could be deactivated if necessary.

Category	Basis
Monitoring object	Trace
Monitoring attribute I of the object	Status of developer trace
Monitoring attribute II of the object	Status of system trace
Responsibility	Centralized system monitoring
Type of monitoring	Automated
Autoreaction method	No

Table 3.25 Monitoring the Trace Functionality

3.7 Memory Management

Using Memory Management, you can assign different SAP memory areas within an SAP instance. The appropriate parameterization enables you to define which memory area is used. During operation hours of an SAP sys-

tem, you should check whether the necessary resources are available to the Memory Management and whether the system is slowed down by paging processes or other bottlenecks due to a lack of resources.

Here, the configuration of the SAP memory areas plays an important role. If the SAP memory areas are not optimally aligned with the system load requirements, the performance will suffer and the end user will no longer be able to work efficiently. It should therefore be your objective to optimize the memory configuration and to avoid program failures caused by memory bottlenecks. Consequently, you must include the different memory areas in your system monitoring model.

Buffers

Applications use buffers in the main memory to temporarily store data. It is necessary to have information about the quality and efficiency of critical buffers in order to maintain and improve a system's performance.

For example, the performance of a system can deteriorate if a table buffer is too small, which can lead to swaps (displacements) and unnecessary reloads of the database. You call it a swap when an object that is to be loaded into the buffer cannot be entirely loaded because the buffer is too small. In such a situation, other objects must be displaced or pushed out of the buffer. In fact, swaps should never occur in a production system.

An attribute for monitoring SAP buffers is the hit ratio. In a production system, you should see a hit ratio of 98% or higher. There are exceptions for the program, for example, the single-record and the import/export buffers which can be below 98%.

Category	Memory management
Monitoring object	SAP table buffer (buffer for table definitions, buffer for field definitions, buffer for table rows, initial values for table rows, short version of table information, buffer for ABAP programs, buffer for menu bars, buffer for dynpros, export/import buffer, calendar buffer, table buffer for generic buffering, table buffer for single-record buffering)

Table 3.26 Monitoring the SAP Buffers

Monitoring attribute I of the object	Hit ratio
Monitoring attribute II of the object	Swap out rate (swaps)
Monitoring attribute III of the object	Free buffer space
Monitoring attribute IV of the object	Space usage for directories
Responsibility	Centralized system monitoring
Type of monitoring	Automated
Autoreaction method	No

Table 3.26 Monitoring the SAP Buffers (cont.)

R/3 Paging Memory, R/3 Roll Memory, R/3 Extended Memory, R/3 Heap Memory

Like the SAP buffers, the R/3 Paging Memory, the R/3 Roll Memory, the R/3 Extended Memory, and the R/3 Heap Memory are separate SAP memory areas. These memory areas are configured for each SAP instance, and system performance plays an important role here, too.

It is highly recommended that you check all the following attributes for the SAP memory areas on a weekly basis, except for the current number of work processes in private mode and the number of restarts of the dialog work processes since startup due to abap/heaplimit being exceeded. If you detect a regular occurrence of this state, you must check the memory configuration or discover whether application errors are the cause.

Category	Memory management
Monitoring object	Memory management
Monitoring attribute I of the object	R/3 Paging Memory: Maximum utilization of paging area since system startup
Monitoring attribute II of the object	R/3 Roll Memory: Maximum utilization of roll area since system startup
Monitoring attribute III of the object	High watermark of extended memory since startup
Monitoring attribute IV of the object	Amount of extended memory in user contexts that are currently active in WPs
Monitoring attribute V of the object	High watermark of heap memory since startup

Monitoring attribute VI of the object	Current number of work processes in PRIV mode
Monitoring attribute VII of the object	Number of dialog-work-process restarts since startup due to abap/heaplimit being exceeded
Responsibility	Centralized system monitoring
Type of monitoring	Automated
Autoreaction method	Yes, for attribute V

Table 3.27 Monitoring Additional SAP Memory Areas

3.8 System Log

All the activities of an application server are documented in a system log. If possible, the syslog messages should be separated according to different topics. For example, we recommend that you treat messages about the basis system, the database, background processing, and communications separately.

In addition, it is advisable to include certain system messages—ones that you know occurred regularly in the past and affected the operation of your systems—into the monitoring process.

Category	System logs
Monitoring object	SAP basis system
Monitoring attribute I of the object	Database
Monitoring attribute II of the object	Background processing
Monitoring attribute III of the object	Spool
Monitoring attribute IV of the object	Application
Monitoring attribute V of the object	Communications
Responsibility	Centralized system monitoring
Type of monitoring	Automated
Autoreaction method	Depending on the system message

Table 3.28 Monitoring the System Logs

3.9 ABAP Runtime Error

If a runtime error or dump occurs during the execution of an ABAP program, the system generates a log entry. This log entry contains detailed information about the problem and it enables you to perform a detailed analysis.

It is not unusual for ABAP runtime errors to occur in a development or testing environment; however, ABAP dumps should be avoided in a production system. If many dumps of the same type occur or if a specific type of dump, which can affect the system operation, is generated in the production system, you must perform a detailed analysis.

Different types of ABAP dumps have different effects on the system operation, for example:

▶ **Memory problems**

Dumps can occur that are related to the memory configuration. This can occur due to an application error or because the overall memory configuration is not ideally adapted to the application's requirements.

▶ **Syntax errors**

Programs that are modified or newly developed should be tested in the testing system for syntax errors and compatibility problems, both during the development phase and upon completion. For example, during these tests, you can check whether the definition of a variable is missing, a comma or a parenthesis was forgotten in the program, or if a runtime error occurred. If the testing is not properly done in the testing system, problems can occur later in the production system. This means that programs containing syntax errors that haven't been eliminated previously will certainly fail during operation and have to be re-engineered, which will ultimately restrict your ability to use the application.

▶ **Transport errors**

Let's look at an example.

During the execution of a program, a function module cannot be found. The ABAP runtime error reads as follows:

```
CALL_FUNCTION_NOT_FOUND
The function module „XYZ" does not exist.
```

In this example, function module XYZ was called. However, it can't be found in the function library. This may occur for several reasons, one of which could be a transport error. This means that you need to check whether transports were unsuccessfully imported into the system recently. If that's the case, you must determine whether the transport concept itself has inherent problems.

▶ **Authorization problems**

If a user sucessfully logs on to a system, it doesn't necessarily mean that he or she can access all its different functions. An authorization concept would describe the access rights of every user within the system. For example, the concept could specify access rights for reporting, specific files, and tables.

The authorization concept prevents users from carrying out activities in the system, which could cause problems or even disrupt the entire flow of business activities within a company.

For example, if a dialog user tries to run a report that calls additional reports and function modules which, in turn, run in the same dialog and involve Remote Function Calls (RFCs) calls, this can evoke runtime error RFC_NO_AUTHORITY, provided the user has only limited or perhaps no authorization for RFC calls.

Category	ABAP runtime error
Monitoring object	ABAP short dumps
Monitoring attribute of the object	Number of short dumps
Responsibility	Centralized system monitoring
Type of monitoring	Automated
Autoreaction method	No

Table 3.29 Monitoring ABAP Dumps

3.10 User Monitoring—System Security

Every company wants to stay in control of its systems. This objective involves the idea of preventing unauthorized users from getting on the system via unnoticed accesses. Needless to say, there is no absolute secure system landscape to prevent attacks from the outside. Computers and applications such as operating systems are made by humans and security considerations are often quickly discarded because of idleness or lack of attentiveness.

We distinguish between two areas of security: the security of the machines themselves and possible attacks from the network or the Internet. Both these areas of security require you to take precautionary measures.

For example, an authorization concept ensures the security of the systems. According to their roles, the system users should be granted the relevant authorizations—and only those. Another aspect is the creation of secure passwords. Usually administrators are much more aware of this security problem than the „normal" users who often tend to use passwords that stem from their social environment and don't contain any cryptic letter combinations.

Do you know how secure the programs are that you use? Actually, you can never be sure that your software doesn't pose any risks. Outside attackers will always try to exploit program weaknesses. In the final analysis, this means that you should also check the passwords of all users regularly to determine whether they are satisfactory.

You should regularly check how many users have tried to log on to a particular system—and not only for purely statistical reasons. It is far more important to identify the number of failed logons as well as the number of locks due to incorrect logon details. A large number of failed logons might indicate that an outsider is systematically trying to enter your system. Additionally, you must ensure that users who repeatedly fail to log on successfully are locked at the right time. Table 3.30 shows some possible monitoring attributes that you can include in the default system monitoring process.

Category	User monitoring
Monitoring object	Logons
Monitoring attribute I of the object	Successful logon of a user
Monitoring attribute II of the object	Failed logon of a user
Monitoring attribute III of the object	Locking of a user due to failed logon
Monitoring attribute IV of the object	RFC/CPIC logon successful
Monitoring attribute V of the object	RFC/CPIC logon failed

Responsibility	Centralized system monitoring
Type of monitoring	Automated
Autoreaction method	No

Table 3.30 Monitoring SAP System Logons

The second aspect to consider when talking about system security is network security. A number of tools can help you to monitor and inspect the network traffic. For example, some tools can „eavesdrop" on the data traffic. Other tools can help you to check specific services such as open ports of machines or those within networks.

3.11   Additional SAP Components

In addition to the R/3-related kernel, other components could be in use too, but this depends on the individual solution. When defining an appropriate monitoring concept for these components, you should ask yourself the following questions:

▶ How important is the availability of the component for the availability of my business processes?

▶ Which performance criteria does the component have to meet in order not to affect my business processes?

▶ Which technical details of the component help me draw conclusions about the status of my business processes?

▶ To what extent do certain monitoring objects of a component affect my business processes?

▶ What measures can be taken for the individual monitoring objects in the case of an emergency?

liveCache Operating Status

Let's look at the SAP APO example of our company, Toys Inc.

In addition to the APO database, a liveCache must be part of the system. If the liveCache fails, the APO system will no longer be functional. Therefore, the availability of the liveCache is as important as that of the APO database. Therefore, the availability of the liveCache is a very important monitoring object.

Depending on the business process, the APO solution can be operated with or without an optimizer. Their availability is only of importance if you use optimizers in your business processes. Therefore, whether you need a monitoring object for the availability of the optimizers is really dependent on your business processes. In the sample scenario with Toys Inc., we don't use optimizers.

Category	liveCache
Monitoring object	Status
Monitoring attribute of the object	Current operating status of liveCache kernel process
Responsibility	Centralized system monitoring
Type of monitoring	Automated
Autoreaction method	Yes

Table 3.31 Monitoring the liveCache Status

liveCache Memory Management and Data Backup

SAP liveCache is a type of database instance based on SAP's database technology. Like every other database, liveCache contains technical components that are required to ensure backup and stability. For example, to avoid a liveCache standstill because of completely full log volumes, you must perform a log backup provided that at least one complete data backup of this database is available. Therefore, we recommend that you run a daily backup.

To avoid a liveCache standstill, you have to monitor both the freely available data area and the log area. It is equally important to monitor the last data backup, because this is the only way to avoid a loss of data if it has to be recovered due to hardware or software problems.

Category	liveCache
Monitoring object	Memory management
Monitoring attribute I of the object	Used data area of data volumes
Monitoring attribute II of the object	Used log area of log volumes
Monitoring attribute III of the object	Status of automatic log backup
Responsibility	Centralized system monitoring
Type of monitoring	Automated
Autoreaction method	No

Table 3.32 Monitoring the liveCache Memory Management

Category	liveCache
Monitoring object	Backup
Monitoring attribute of the object	Last successfully completed data backup
Responsibility	Centralized system monitoring
Type of monitoring	Automated
Autoreaction method	No

Table 3.33 Monitoring the liveCache Backup Runs

Certain performance-relevant criteria enable you to better understand the current status of your system. Not only does a slow system frustrate the users, it can also lead to a system breakdown, which would have a substantial effect on the business processes. Consequently, the required throughput cannot be reached anymore; otherwise, the users would have to work overtime. This could even result in financial losses for the company.

Data Cache Hit Ratio

For a liveCache to work properly, the accesses to liveCache data have to take place in the main memory, and only there. I/O accesses should be avoided, because every access to the hard disk slows down the processing speed.

One area of the main memory is the data cache. The data cache contains all object management system (OMS) data. If the data cache is too small to hold all the relevant data, its pages will be written into the data volumes. You should always try to ensure that this doesn't happen. An indicator that shows you whether all OMS data was successfully read from the data cache or from the hard disk is the hit ratio. The hit ratio value should not be lower than 99.8%. If it's lower, you must check the overall data-cache utilization. If the value is exactly 100%, the data cache might be too small. But this is only one possible cause, which means that you must check the actual size of the data cache.

The aforementioned considerations show you how important system monitoring is, and also, how important it is to define measures that must be taken in case of an emergency—before you design your monitoring model. This is the only way to avoid unwanted system downtime.

Optimizer Statistics

The SQL Optimizer controls the handling of accesses to tables in the liveCache. It gets the necessary information for its control activity from the optimizer statistics, which are updated on a regular basis. A regular execution of optimizer statistics ensures an optimal handling of SQL statements which, in turn, improves the system performance and which is why you should schedule the table statistics at least once a week.

Category	liveCache
Monitoring object	Performance
Monitoring attribute I of the object	Data cache hit ratio
Monitoring attribute II of the object	Last update of SQL optimizer statistics
Responsibility	Centralized system monitoring
Type of monitoring	Automated
	No

Table 3.34 Monitoring the liveCache Performance Criteria

3.12   Database

The world of IT today is not conceivable without the use of database management systems (DBMS). Without a DBMS, we wouldn't be able to oversee or deal with the vast amount of data that has to be processed and evaluated. To ensure availability, database integrity, performance, redundancy, and data security, it is necessary to implement a regular database monitoring.

If you monitor the database regularly, you'll get information about the database during operation, and you will be notified about problems and can avoid critical situations by using proactive measures. In addition, you will be able to identify and analyze problems and gather the necessary information about the settings of the database system. To monitor a DBMS, you should include indicators such as the database size, the quality of the database buffers, possible storage space problems, and the database performance.

There are various providers of database systems on the market, and each DBMS is based on a database model, of which there are several. We usually distinguish between hierarchical, relational, and object-oriented database models. Irrespective of the database model you use, you

can specify a general approach for monitoring a DBMS. Therefore, in the following sections, we will mention those monitoring objects that are common to all database systems and can therefore be applied to our sample company.

Database and Table Growth

The growth of a database depends on the number of business transactions within a specific period. You can be certain of one thing: Each new transaction will increase the amount of transactional and master data in the database. While the maintenance effort increases, the data retrieval becomes increasingly less efficient, and consequently, the performance of business transactions may be impacted. This degradation of performance is eventually noticed by the users. You can counteract all these problems by implementing proactive measures such as the regular control of the database growth.

One possible way to increase system performance is to monitor the ever-growing amount of data by implementing better CPUs and a higher storage capacity. However, this can be fairly expensive. Therefore, it would be preferable to determine how you can decrease the database size. For example, you might think of archiving, compressing, or reorganizing your data in to reduce the size of the database.

Category	Database
Monitoring object	Database
Monitoring attribute of the object	Database size and growth
Responsibility	Centralized system monitoring
Type of monitoring	Automated
Autoreaction method	No

Table 3.35 Monitoring the Database Growth

Category	Database
Monitoring object	Tables
Monitoring attribute of the object	Table size and growth
Responsibility	Centralized system monitoring
Type of monitoring	Automated
Autoreaction method	No

Table 3.36 Monitoring the Table Growth

Database Buffers

Every database contains different buffers that are used to store both database management information and user data in the main memory. The use of buffers in the main memory reduces the number of accesses to the hard disk, which, in turn, shortens the access time for objects that are already in the buffer. I/O accesses should be avoided because every access to the hard disk slows down the processing speed.

For the database performance, the quality of access to database buffers is extremely relevant to performance. Depending on the database system, there are different threshold values of which your system shouldn't fall short. In an SAP database instance, the database buffer hit ratio is 99%.

Category	Database
Monitoring object	Database buffers
Monitoring attribute of the object	Database buffer quality
Responsibility	Centralized system monitoring
Type of monitoring	Automated
Autoreaction method	No

Table 3.37 Monitoring the Database Buffer

Optimizer Statistics

To execute a SQL statement, there are typically several file-access paths. A database optimizer decides which access path will be taken, and to make this decision, it needs table statistics. These statistics enable the optimizer to choose the best strategy to find the data. Outdated statistics affect the performance of the database instance.

Category	Database
Monitoring object	Optimizer
Monitoring attribute of the object	Last update of optimizer statistics
Responsibility	Centralized system monitoring
Type of monitoring	Automated
Autoreaction method	No

Table 3.38 Monitoring the Optimizer Statistics

I/O Activities—Hard Disk Accesses

For an optimal performance, you must ensure equal loads for each hard disk. If some of the hard disks are exposed to higher loads, a situation indicated by a higher hard-disk utilization, an I/O bottleneck could be the result. This is reflected in longer wait and response times for I/O operations on the highly frequented disks. You can avoid I/O bottlenecks by better distributing the data to the all the disks in your system.

Category	Database
Monitoring object	Hard disks
Monitoring attribute of the object	Wait and response times of I/O operations
Responsibility	Centralized system monitoring
Type of monitoring	Automated
Autoreaction method	No

Table 3.39 Monitoring I/O Activities

Storage Management

Every database instance consists of physical storage units—disks—to which all system and application data is written. To avoid a database failure, you must control the free disk space capacity on a regular basis. If you foresee that the hard disk resources will soon reach their capacity limit, due to a constantly growing amount of data, they must be extended.

Category	Database
Monitoring object	Storage management
Monitoring attribute of the object	Disk utilization
Responsibility	Centralized system monitoring
Type of monitoring	Automated
Autoreaction method	No

Table 3.40 Monitoring the Disk Utilization

Data Backup

One of the major tasks of a system administrator is to ensure that data is continuously backed up. By running regular backups, you can at least minimize the impact of hardware defects, damages caused by natural forces, or even the loss of data due to unintentional delete or overwrite processes. Basically, a data backup is the only way to recover data. You won't be able to see how useful it is until the very moment when you have to recover lost data.

To avoid a loss of data and to ensure that the current data can actually be recovered, you must monitor the data backup process. For example, if you have to perform a data recovery and during the recovery process you notice that the last successful backup was more than a week ago, your data is no longer up-to-date. All changes to data that have been done since the last successful backup will be lost.

Category	Database
Monitoring object	Data backup
Monitoring attribute of the object	Last successfully completed data backup
Responsibility	Centralized system monitoring
Type of monitoring	Automated
Autoreaction method	No

Table 3.41 Monitoring the Data Backup

3.13 Communication Interfaces

The exchange of data between two SAP systems, or an SAP system and a third-party system, or between two third-party systems, happens through a communication interface. For example, a data exchange takes place if an availability check is performed in the supplier system due to a customer request for a specific material; a data exchange also takes place when order confirmations, delivery notes, or invoices are sent to customers. Regardless of whether the data transfer is synchronous or asynchronous, you must ensure that it is transferred properly and that orders arriving in the target system are processed correctly.

To ensure a smooth data exchange, you need specific information for your monitoring processes depending on the communication technology you use (for example, RFC, IDoc, and BAPI). First, this means that it is necessary to become familiar with communication technology in general in order to determine which monitoring objects should be included in the monitoring process.

In the system monitoring of our sample company, Toys Inc., the transactional RFC, and the queued RFC play an important role. Both the transactional and the queued RFCs are variants of the remote function calls that are used to make data transfers between different SAP systems more reliable and secure.

tRFC (transactional Remote Function Call)

The transfer of data between separate SAP systems or between an SAP system and an external component is enabled by the tRFC function. tRFC stands for transactional Remote Function Call, which means that, similar to database transactions, the ACID rules apply.

▶ **Atomicity**

If an error occurs during a transaction, all changes done to the database until this moment will be undone. This means that either all changes that a transaction does to a database are applied or none are applied.

▶ **Consistency**

All integrity conditions of the database are adhered to, that is, on the basis of a consistent status of the database, the result of any transaction also has to be a consistent database status.

▶ **Isolation**

Every transaction runs as an isolated independent transaction. This implies that for each transaction, the database only makes data available that is part of a consistent state.

▶ **Durability**

It is ensured that after a successful commit, changes are stored in the database.

This means that every function module sent to the target system is executed exactly once. Although tRFC does increase the reliability of data transfers substantially, it also contains some drawbacks. For example, it cannot be ensured that the sequence of logical units of work (LUWs) specified in an application will be adhered to. It can only be guaranteed that all LUWs will be transferred at some point.

During a transfer, different errors statuses can occur, for example, a network or communication problem that occurs during the transfer of a LUW. This error status can be identified by the CPICERR error message. If the system returns the SYSFAIL error message, it means that a serious error occurred in the target system during the processing of the LUW, which will then terminate. If the sending system tries to send an LUW directly without using any outbound queues and there's no free work process available, the system will return the SYSLOAD error message.

Category	Interfaces
Monitoring object	Transactional RFC calls
Monitoring attribute I of the object	Calls in CPICERR state
Monitoring attribute II of the object	Calls in SYSFAIL state
Monitoring attribute III of the object	Calls in SYSLOAD state
Responsibility	Centralized system monitoring
Type of monitoring	Automated
Autoreaction method	No

Table 3.42 Monitoring tRFC

qRFC (queued Remote Function Call)

In order to counteract the disadvantages of tRFC, a serialization of tRFC takes place via queues, which is called queued RFC (qRFC). qRFC is an enhancement of tRFC that groups tRFC calls into outbound and inbound queues. If you use qRFC with outbound queues (see Table 3.43), you can ensure that tRFC calls will be executed in the target system in exactly the same sequence as they were added to the queue.

Category	Interfaces
Monitoring object	qRFC outbound queues
Monitoring attribute of the object	Status of queue
Responsibility	Centralized system monitoring
Type of monitoring	Automated
Autoreaction method	No

Table 3.43 Monitoring qRFC Outbound Queues

If you use qRFC with inbound queues (see Table 3.44), you can ensure that incoming calls for a specific queue will be executed in the sequence in which they arrive.

qRFC is used frequently in the Core Interface (CIF) for data transfers between APO and R/3 systems.

Whether a transmission request is processed successfully or unsuccessfully, it is monitored in the outbound and inbound queues.

Category	Interfaces
Monitoring object	qRFC inbound queues
Monitoring attribute of the object	Status of queue
Responsibility	Centralized system monitoring
Type of monitoring	Automated
Autoreaction method	No

Table 3.44 Monitoring qRFC Inbound Queues

QIN and QOUT Schedulers

On the basis of the currently existing system resources, the QIN Scheduler has to activate as many inbound queues as possible. It includes only those queues that are registered. In addition, the QIN Scheduler can monitor the runtime of a queue at the end of an LUW execution in order to pause it, if necessary, so that other queues can be processed as well. The QIN Scheduler controls the processing of incoming tRFC and qRFC calls within a specific client.

You can use the QOUT Scheduler to avoid overloading the target system with too many transmission requests. This tool helps you to limit the maximum number of parallel connections (tRFC/qRFC) for a specific connection so that the maximum number of RFCs can be controlled. In this context, we recommend that you monitor the status of the QOUT Scheduler.

Your system monitoring model should include a regular check of the status of the QIN and QOUT Schedulers. They control and monitor an equal distribution of RFC resources, which enables you to avoid resource and performance problems in an SAP system.

Category	Interfaces
Monitoring object	QIN Scheduler
Monitoring attribute of the object	Inbound scheduler error
Responsibility	Centralized system monitoring
Type of monitoring	Automated
Autoreaction method	No

Table 3.45 Monitoring the QIN Scheduler

Category	Interfaces
Monitoring object	QOUT Scheduler
Monitoring attribute of the object	Outbound scheduler error
Responsibility	Centralized system monitoring
Type of monitoring	Automated
Autoreaction method	No

Table 3.46 Monitoring the QOUT Scheduler

3.14 Self-Monitoring of Monitoring Tools

To ensure the proper operation of your systems, you not only need to monitor the individual components of your system landscape but to regularly check whether the monitoring tools themselves run properly. If they don't function, there can be no automated monitoring.

Since SAP Solution Manager is the monitoring tool used in our example, we will describe certain criteria in the following sections that are related to this tool. Additionally you will find information about some prerequisites for using SAP Solution Manager.

Availability of SAP Solution Manager Systems

Note that you also have to ensure the accessibility and availability of the centralized monitoring system. Therefore, when designing your monitoring concept, you must consider the following:

▶ How do you want to monitor the centralized monitoring system?

▶ Which monitoring objects and attributes have to be included in the monitoring process?

▶ Which monitoring procedures are activated in case the monitoring tool fails?

As with all the other SAP components, you could configure the availability monitoring via the system availability and the application server availability. This can be done using the availability agent CCMSPING.

You can find information about installing and configuring the CCMSPING agent at SAP Service Marketplace using the following quick link: *Monitoring · System Monitoring and Alert Management · Media Library · Documentation · Availability Monitoring and Agent CCMSPING*.

Category	SAP Solution Manager
Monitoring object I	System availability
Monitoring object II	Instance availability
Monitoring attribute of the object I	Availability per system
Monitoring attribute of the object II	Status of instance availability
Responsibility	Centralized system monitoring
Type of monitoring	Automated
Autoreaction method	Yes

Table 3.47 Monitoring System and Instance Availability of SAP Solution Manager

Monitoring the CCMS Monitoring Architecture

The monitoring architecture of the Computing Center Management System (CCMS) provides an infrastructure to gather and manage system information. For the system-monitoring process, SAP Solution Manager uses functions of this monitoring architecture, which means that without the monitoring architecture SAP Solution Manager is not functional at all.

To collect data for different monitoring objects, data collectors are available that send data for monitored objects to the monitoring architecture. The monitoring architecture constantly compares the measurement values provided by the data collectors with the threshold values and triggers an alarm when the measurement values are above or below the thresholds. If the data collectors don't function properly, monitoring is not possible.

Category	Monitoring architecture
Monitoring object	Data collectors
Monitoring attribute of the object	Information about possible data collector problems
Responsibility	Centralized system monitoring
Type of monitoring	Automated
Autoreaction method	Yes

Table 3.48 Monitoring the Data Collectors

CCMS Agents

CCMS agents are self-contained processes with one RFC interface to a central monitoring system and one to the shared memory. CCMS agents enable you to include SAP components that don't have an ABAP interface to your monitoring system.

CCMS can collect monitoring data about the system to be monitored, send this data to the central monitoring system, and save it in a cache for a faster display or trigger a central autoreaction method.

With push technology, the central monitoring system doesn't automatically request monitoring data from the monitored system on a regular basis; instead, an agent transfers this data to the central monitoring system as needed. To use push technology, SAP Web AS 6.10 or higher must be installed in the central monitoring system, whose performance will improve substantially.

Depending on the type of system you want to monitor, you can use one of three different CCMS agents.

Agent	Task
SAPCCMSR	Monitoring components on which no SAP instance is active
SAPCCM4X	Monitoring SAP systems from SAP Basis Release 4.x
SAPCM3X	Monitoring SAP Basis Release 3.x systems using CCMS monitoring architecture

Table 3.49 CCMS Agents

We will not describe how to install, register, and use the agents, but you can find a detailed documentation in SAP Service Marketplace using quick link: *Monitoring · System Monitoring and Alert Management · Monitoring in Detail · CCMS Agents Properties, Installation and Operation*.

SAPCCMSR

The SAPCCMSR agent monitors both SAP and non-SAP components on which no SAP instance is active, such as databases without SAP instance or operating-system components.

SAPCCM4X

You can use the SAPCCM4X agent to monitor SAP systems of Release 4.x or higher. This agent provides an alternative connection path for monitoring information about an SAP instance in the shared memory. In this context, no free-work process is needed to write and read the monitoring information, therefore, monitoring data

can be collected irrespective of the status of the SAP instance.

What happens if the agent is inactive and unable to send data to the central monitoring system? In this case, the central monitoring system will at first automatically attempt to read the data of the system being monitored through the RFC connection in the CCMS agent. If the agent is not active, the monitoring data of the SAP instance being monitored will be read by the standard RFC as before.

SAPCM3X

The SAPCM3X agent permits the monitoring of SAP instances of SAP basis Release 3.x through CCMS monitoring architecture.

The SAPCCMSR and SAPCCM4X agents are used in our Toys Inc example:

▶ **SAPCCMSR**

This agent is installed on the host where the non-SAP WAMA solution is running. This is the only way of using SAP tools to receive information about the operating system's resources workload.

▶ **SAPCCM4X**

In addition, SAPCCM4X agent technologies are used for the R/3 system and the SCM system. This agent technology is used in order to leverage the push technique described above. This means the monitoring data is sent from the agents to the central monitoring system, and the central monitoring system performance is ensured.

Category	CCMS agents
Monitoring object I	SAPCCMSR
Monitoring object II	SAPCCM4X
Monitoring attribute of objects I and II	Availability
Responsibility	Centralized system monitoring
Type of monitoring	Automated
Autoreaction method	Yes

Table 3.50 Monitoring the CCMS agents

3.15 Monitoring System Components Without an SAP Instance

Components outside the SAP environment must also be monitored. Some manufacturers provide an individual monitoring tool compatible with their application. An advantage of this practice is that these tools are generally available for immediate use with little difficulty. The disadvantage is that the centralized monitoring function becomes irrelevant during the simultaneous use of several monitoring tools in a heterogeneous system environment A useful solution at this point is the provision of a central monitoring tool to send monitoring data from non-SAP components to the centralized monitoring tool via interfaces.

SAP similarly provides tools to monitor non-SAP components. The SAPCCMSR agent is one of these tools. This agent monitors components that have no active SAP instance. It compiles data and sends it to the centralized monitoring system. Log files can be integrated into the monitoring process, as can OS components, or independent databases along with their components. To do this, Toys Inc. can use SAPCCMSR agents and, if necessary, develop further interfaces.

Log File

It is possible to monitor log files from SAP and non-SAP components. Monitoring is carried out through the SAPCCMSR CCMS agent in components that are not part of the SAP environment. A log file agent is integrated into these agents and monitors log files according to specific search templates. Therefore, searches can be carried out in any text file for any text sample. These can be assigned alerts and the results can be displayed in the alert monitor.

The following log file types can be monitored by CCMS agents:
- Log files that are continuously described by the application and therefore constantly increase
- Log files that are rewritten by the application after each restart under the same names.
- Log files that are created every time by the application with new names

Category	Log file
Monitoring object	<Name of the log file>
Monitoring attribute of the object	<Search template>
Responsibility	Centralized system monitoring
Type of monitoring	Automated
Autoreaction method	No

Table 3.51 Monitoring Log Files

Operating System

Monitoring the non-SAP operating systems is another key task. Depending on which monitoring objects—described in Section 3.2—are involved, these objects must also be considered in system components outside of the SAP environment during the monitoring process. The SAPCCMSR CCMS agent is also used for this. After successfully installing the agents, information on the file system, the CPU, and memory workload etc. is displayed in the CCMS monitoring architecture.

3.16 Documenting Changes in the System Monitoring

The previous sections described the content of the monitoring concept. You have learned about the typical components of a monitoring concept. The issue of how the process looks when changes are made in the monitoring still remains to be discussed. For instance, you can integrate new monitoring objects into the monitoring process or adapt specific threshold values for a monitoring object, or change the troubleshooting procedure for an object. Many other kinds of changes are possible as well.

Change protocols in system monitoring are extremely important if an outsourcer takes over monitoring the system landscape. Service level agreements on system maintenance are generally set at the beginning of a business relationship between the outsourcer and the customer. They form the basis for establishing the criteria that can play a role in system monitoring. If, after production begins, it turns out that the criteria established does not fulfill the agreement by 100%, the criteria must be reworked.

Errors can also occur in the adaptation process. They can be found and traced more easily by using documentation.

Who Is Responsible for Documenting the Changes?

To prevent individuals from making arbitrary changes to the system monitoring, it is critical that an administrator is appointed. Changes will be suggested to this person. With expert support, it will be decided whether or not to implement these changes.

What Does a Change Protocol Look Like?

A change protocol must be simple and straightforward. You should include the following information in the documentation:

▶ The reason for the change and a brief description
▶ The individual(s) who made the suggestion
▶ The individual(s) who supported the administrator in making the decision
▶ The implementation process effort
▶ The effects of the changes when introduced
▶ The date for adapting it to the monitoring system
▶ The individual who will carry out the customization in the monitoring system

What Does the Process Description Look Like?

Another critical step is the creation of a process description. This should contain a procedure for making changes in the system monitoring model. When a central monitoring system has been introduced for the first time, changes will almost certainly become necessary as staff gains experience on technical and organizational levels. You should ensure that individuals involved in system monitoring are aware of the changes made to the process.

4 System Monitoring Using SAP Solution Manager 3.1

This chapter describes how system monitoring is set up in SAP Solution Manager in relation to the monitoring architecture of the Computer Center Management System (CCMS). You will develop an understanding of the technical prerequisites in the central monitoring system and the monitored systems. A description of SAP Solution Manager and the system-monitoring implementation process follows. We will also describe the implementation process for the central autoreaction method in the central monitoring system.

4.1 Computer Center Management System

The monitoring architecture of the CCMS provides every SAP system with a flexible and globally usable infrastructure that monitors the entire IT landscape and offers fast, reliable reports on any problems that may occur. SAP Solution Manager monitoring techniques are based on CCMS functions. Its functions include monitoring the hardware, database, SAP basis components, and availability monitoring as well as analysis and data collection methods. That means that SAP Solution Manager cannot function as a monitoring tool without CCMS monitoring architecture.

4.2 Prerequisites

Before system monitoring can be set up in SAP Solution Manager, we will summarize which general activities and prerequisites are necessary for the implementation process. There are more prerequisites for a few additional monitoring objects. For example, for availability monitoring, you also need CCMSPING agents. Reference will be made to these and other monitoring objects during the implementation processes in the corresponding sections.

> **Satellite Systems**
>
> Systems connected to the SAP Solution Manager, which are to be monitored, are referred to as "satellite systems." We will use this term throughout the remainder of this chapter.

Installing SAP Solution Manager

The first step is to install SAP Solution Manager 3.1. You will find the document on how to install SAP Solution Manager 3.1 in SAP Service Marketplace. You can download this document at *www.service.sap.com/inst-guides · SAP Components · SAP Solution Manager · Release 3.1 · Installation Guides*.

Depending on which operating system and database SAP Solution Manager will run, choose the corresponding installation manual. Figure 4.1 provides you with an overview of the current installation documents for SAP Solution Manager in SAP Service Marketplace, documents that were made available for the operating system and the database after the Solution Manager was released. Carry out the individual steps in accordance with the document that you select. This book does not delve into further detail on installing SAP Solution Manager 3.1.

Support Packages

When using SAP Solution Manager 3.1, you need an SAP CRM 3.1 server for exclusive use of the Solution Manager central system. In addition, SAP BASIS and SAP_ABA with the relevant support-package level are prerequisites (see Table 4.1).

It is generally advisable that you install the latest support package, which contains corrections and upgrades.

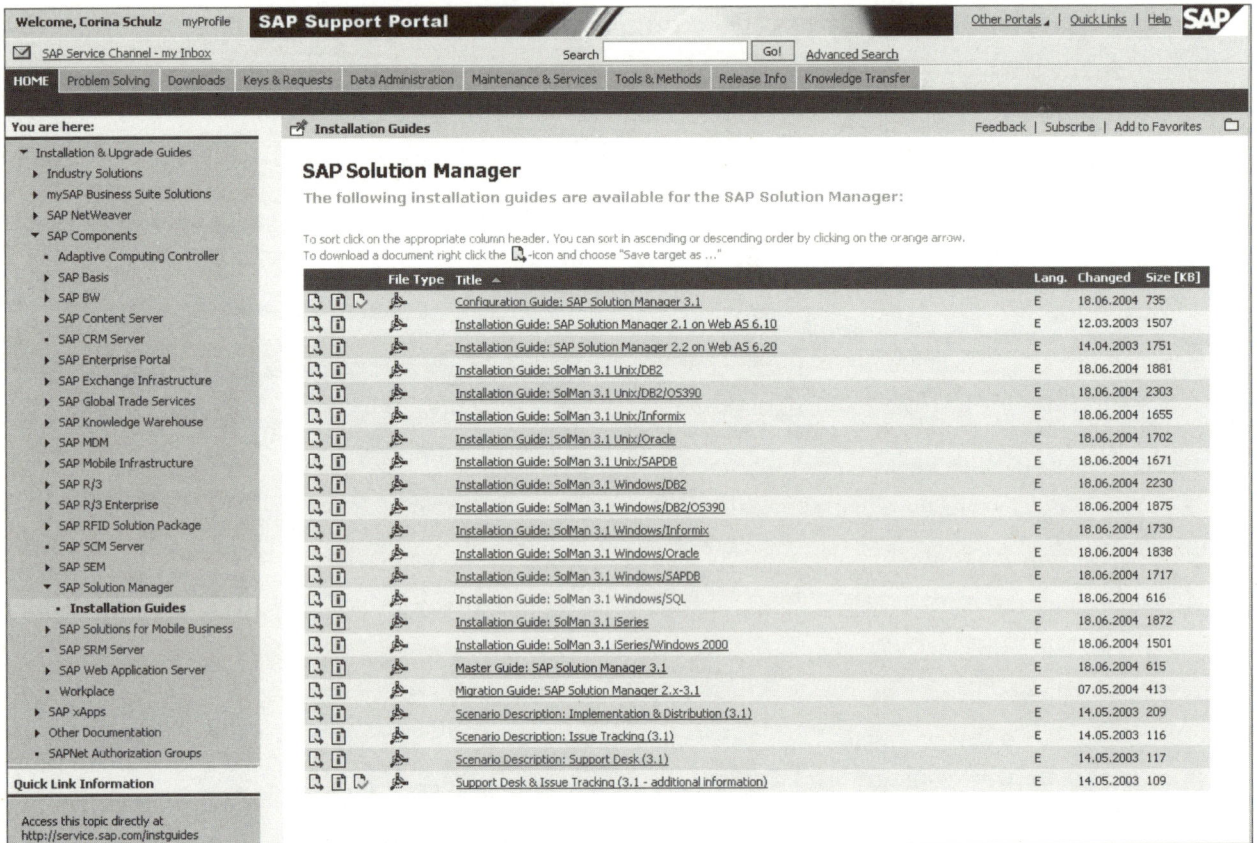

Figure 4.1   SAP Service Marketplace—Overview of SAP Solution Manager Installation Documents

Solution Manager System	Software Components	Minimum Support Package Level
SAP CRM 3.1h	SAP_BASIS	SP28
	SAP_ABA	SP28
	BBPCRM	SP06
Solution Manager 3.1	ST 310	SP04
	ST-SER 310	SP05

Table 4.1   Minimum Support Package Level for Using SAP Solution Manager

Add-on SAP Solution Manager

SAP Solution Manager is provided as an add-on component for implementation and operation. The add-on ID is ST. Up to and including Release ST 220, the Solution Manager is supplied with SAP Web Application Server (software components SAP_BASIS and SAP_ABA). Since Release ST 310, it is provided as a complete installation. The maintenance of the ST add-on is done via support packages. You can find the ST support packages in SAP Service Marketplace: *www.service.sap.com/patches • SAP-Software Distribution Center • Download • SAP Support*

Packages and Patches • Entry by Application Group • SAP Technology Components • SAP Solution Manager.

Further Add-Ons

Further add-ons are available depending on the functionalities to be used in SAP Solution Manager. Some of these add-ons will be explained in the following sections. Please note that add-on installations can only be installed on components of specific releases.

▶ **PI_Basis—SAP Basis Plug-in**

The SAP Basis Plug-in is a software component that can be installed on an SAP Web AS or any other product that runs on SAP_BASIS 620 and SAP_ABA 620 or higher. It facilitates the communication between different application systems that can run on different platforms. Note that the SAP Basis Plug-in requires the SAP R/3 Plug-in. Therefore, when you upgrade the SAP R/3 Plug-in, SAP Basis Plug-in must also be upgraded.

► **ST-ICO—SAP Solution Manager Implementation Content**

The ST-ICO add-on provides content, which is used in the SAP Solution Manager to implement SAP solutions. This content consists of descriptions and integrated configuration information for business scenarios supported by SAP, as well as product-specific information for projects being implemented and already in operation, along with information about upgrading an SAP system landscape. Project information is sorted according to the usual phases of the project lifecycle.

► **ST-PI—SAP Solution Tools Plug-in**

The ST-PI add-on contains the latest versions of the following functions:

- ► Data collection elements
- ► Transaction SDCC (Service Data Control Center)
- ► Transaction SQLR (SQL Trace Interpreter)
- ► Function modules that use Transaction SMSY to read system information.

SDCC and SQLR are contained in ST-PI for SAP Release 4.0B to 4.6D. Since Release 6.10 of SAP Web AS, the transactions are contained in SAP Basis Standard. Corrections and new versions are supplied in Basis support packages.

► **ST-SER—SAP Solution Services**

The ST-SER add-on provides content, which can be used in SAP Solution Manager for the implementation, operation, and monitoring of SAP solutions.

► **ST-SUP—SAP Solution Manager Support Desk**

The ST-SUP add-on has been available since Release 3.1. This add-on contains control data for SAP Solution Manager support desk configuration. It is based on CRM 3.1 (BBPCRM). Note that SAP CRM 3.1 is modified when the ST-SUP add-on is imported. To avoid conflicts, support packages for SAP CRM 3.1 can only be imported with Conflict Resolution Transport (CRT).

► **ST-A/PI—Application Service Tools**

The ST-A/PI add-on contains application-specific tools—the ST14 application monitor and report RTCCTOOL. These tools must be installed prior to an SAP service such as SAP EarlyWatch Check. From Release 4.0B onwards, SAP systems contain these application-specific tools in ST-A/PI. ST14 and RTCCTOOL are only supplied as separate Sapserv 3-7 transports with the older R/3 3.0D-3.1I releases.

Add-on	Description
PI_BASIS	SAP Basis Plug-in
ST	SAP Solution Manager tool
ST-ICO	SAP Solution Manager Implementation Content
ST-PI	SAP Solution Tools Plug-in
ST-SER	SAP Solution Manager Service Tools
ST-SUP	SAP Solution Manager Support Desk
ST-A/PI	Application Service Tools

Table 4.2 Add-ons Contained in the Setup in Release 3.10 (Default Release)

ST-PI and ST-A/PI

Use the current versions of ST-PI and ST-A/PI to monitor the systems. Implement these add-ons in SAP Solution Manager as well as in the satellite systems.

SAP Solution Manager Control

In order to be able to process graphics in the SAP Solution Manager, an ActiveX Control (OCX) must be installed on the local host. You will find the current installation program in SAP Service Marketplace under *www.service.sap.com/solutionmanager* · *Downloads* · *SAP Solution Manager Downloads*.

Note Assistant

The Note Assistant enables you to import ABAP source code corrections from SAP Notes into your SAP system in an easy and convenient manner. We recommend that you install the Note Assistant on all satellite systems as well as the SAP Solution Manager system. The Note Assistant is part of SAP's standard functionality since Release 6.10 of SAP Web AS.

SAP Solution Manager System Users

You should create a user in your SAP Solution Manager system in order to maintain and administer it.

We recommend that you create a temporary user (see Table 4.3), who has all the necessary authorizations required to carry out an initial configuration in the system. Once this configuration is complete, you should delete this user from your system.

User	Profile
SOLMANINST	SAP_ALL
	SAP_NEW

Table 4.3   The SOLMANINST Temporary User and Its SAP Solution Manager Profile

You also need a user who can perform administrative tasks such as creating the solution landscape, setting up the monitoring concept, and carrying out background processing.

The user SOLMAN_RFC is an RFC user. This user is responsible for transferring data from the satellite system to SAP Solution Manager.

Table 4.4 lists the roles and profiles that should be set for the users.

User	Type of user	Roles	Profile
SOLMAN	Dialog	SAP_SV_SOLUTION_ MANAGER	S_SDCC_ ADMIN
		SAP_BC_RRR_SAA_ ADMIN	
		SAP_BC_NETWORK_OS_ ADMIN	
SOLMAN_ RFC	System/ CPIC		D_SOLMAN_ RFC

Table 4.4   SAP Solution Manager and Its Roles and Profiles

Satellite System Users

For system monitoring, a user is needed to deliver monitoring data via remote access from the CCMS of the monitored systems to the SAP Solution Manager monitoring system. This user is not automatically created. Therefore, you should create a CSMREG user in each satellite system. The S_CSMREG profile for the CSMREG user contains the following authorizations:

Authorization object	Field	Value
S_CCM_RECV (for Rel. >=4.6X)	ACTVT	P0-P2
	TABLE	*

Authorization object	Field	Value
S_RFC (for all releases)	RFC_TYPE	FUGR
	RFC_NAME	SALC SALF SALH SALS SAL_CACHE_RECEIVE /SDF/* SYST SCSM* /SOMO/BP_MONI /SOMO/MA_ANA /SOMO/MA_DSA URFC (for Rel. >=6.20) RFC1 THFB DSWP_BPM SADB SLCA (for Rel. >=4.6C)
	ACTVT	16
S_RZL_ADM	ACTVT	01

Table 4.5   Authorization Objects for the CSMREG User

In SAP systems from Basis Release 4.6C onwards, select the user type Communications, or enter CPIC in lower release systems.

Operating System Collector—SAPOSCOL

The SAPOSCOL operating system collector should be installed on all monitoring systems. This is an independent program that runs in the background. By default, SAPOSCOL collects current data every 10 seconds on specific operating resources such as memory usage, CPU, and data system utilization.

SAPOSCOL can be used in both SAP and non-SAP systems to monitor operating system resources. In the past, RFCOSCOL had to be installed to monitor external hosts. This functionality has now been integrated into the CCMS agents, which means that you only have to install the relevant CCMS agent on the external host to be monitored. When the agent is registered, an RFC connection, monitoring objects, and table entries for ST06/OS07 are automatically created. In this context, DB2 for z/OS is an exception because RFCOSCOL is still needed for DB performance monitoring. You can find the latest version of SAPOSCOL in SAP Service Marketplace.

4.3 Configuring SAP Solution Manager

Maintaining System Data

A system landscape consists of several systems, each of which, in turn, consists of hardware and software components. Each component contains certain properties. For example, these include system data such as the number of CPUs on a host or the status of a system's SAP Basis support package.

At this point, we would like to reiterate the following advice. First, collect all relevant information on the systems and their components in order to initiate the configuration process in SAP Solution Manager as effectively as possible. With Toys Inc, the required information on the monitoring concept was compiled in Chapter 3.

In SAP Solution Manager, the system data can be automatically created and collected, or manually created and maintained.

► **Automatic data transfer of system data**

Use the automatic data transfer function (Transaction SMSY_SETUP) as shown in Figure 4.2, to gather system data and set up the system landscape from the Landscape Information System (LIS) or the System and Landscape Directory (SLD). This data is used to automatically collect information on hosts, databases, and systems. The automatically identified landscape elements and the related automatically calculated data in the SAP Solution Manager can neither be deleted nor changed when the data source is set at automatic maintenance. In order to process all the data in these landscape elements, you would have to change the data source to manual maintenance. The change is done in the System Landscape Maintenance (Transaction SMSY). Select the system where you want to change it. On the right side under Data Source, you can switch between automatic and manual maintenance.

This book does not explore the setup of system landscapes and maintenance using automatic data transfer.

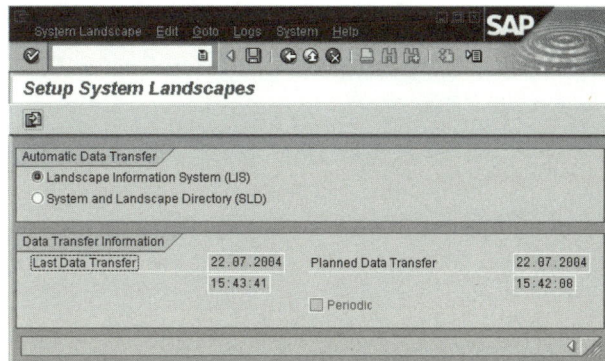

Figure 4.2 SAP Solution Manager 3.1: Setting Up System Landscapes

► **Manual maintenance of system data**

System data can also be inserted and maintained manually. Individual steps to manually create host data, database data, and systems for the SAP systems BLA and BLN and the non-SAP WAMA product used at Toys Inc. will now be described. Please also take note of the section "Product Definition of Non-SAP Products" with regard to the WAMA system. That section is a prerequisite for creating the WAMA system.

Creating Host Data

Call Transaction SMSY (Solution Manager System Landscape).

1. Mark the **Host** landscape component.
2. Select **Landscape Components · Create object · Create host**. A new dialog opens.
3. Enter the host name.
4. Save your entries.
5. Select the host name under the landscape component **Hosts**. On the right-hand side of the screen, you can enter the details of the host. Figure 4.3 illustrates the monitor used to create host data in SMSY.
6. Save your entries.

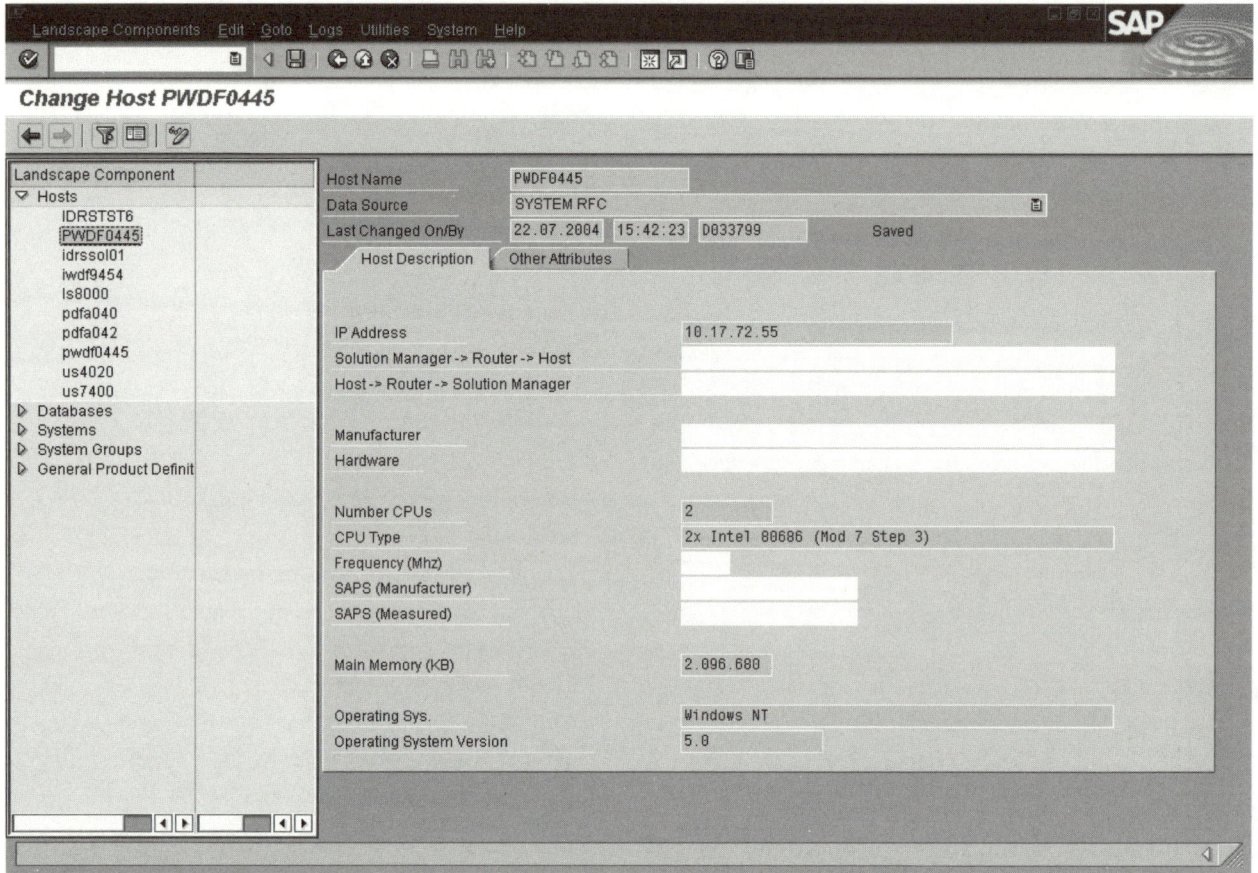

Figure 4.3   Creating Host Data

Creating Database Data

1 Call Transaction SMSY.

2 Select the landscape component **Databases**.

3 Select **Landscape Components · Create object · Create database**. A new dialog opens.

4 Enter the database name.

5 Save your entries.

6 Select the database names under the **Database** landscape component. On the right-hand side of the screen you can enter the database details. Figure 4.4 shows the monitor for creating database data in the SMSY.

7 Save your entries.

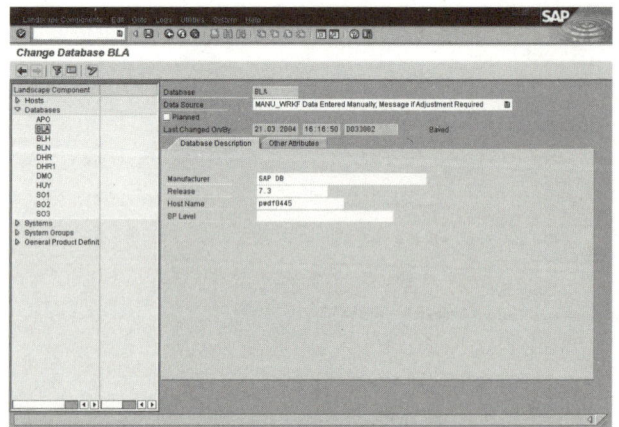

Figure 4.4   Creating Database Data for the BLA System

Creating Systems

1 Call Transaction SMSY.

2 Select the **Systems** landscape component.

3 Select **Landscape Components · Create object · Create system**. A new dialog opens.

4 Insert the System ID as a system name.

5 Select a product and a product version from the input help. If the product is not available, follow the instructions in the next section, "Product Definition of Non-SAP Products."

6 Save your entries.

7 Select the **System ID** under the landscape component **Systems · <Product>** and if necessary set a different ABAP-based main instance on the **System Description** tab as **Relevant** or set several non-ABAP main instances as **Relevant**. Only main instances marked as relevant can be displayed in the operational process in your solution landscape as shown in Figure 4.5. In this case, the APO server as an ABAP instance and the liveCache are set as relevant.

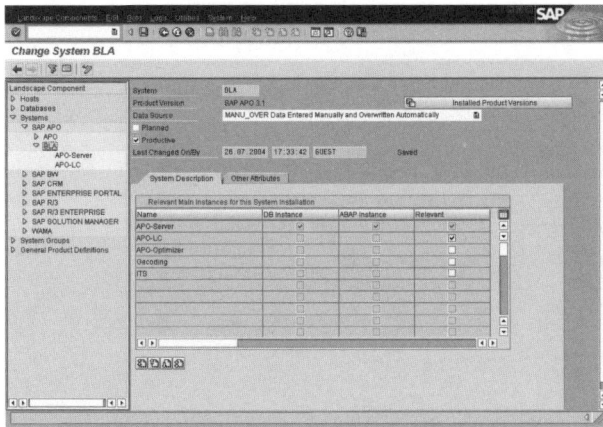

Figure 4.5 Creating Systems for the BLA System

8 Compile more information on the system as necessary.

9 Save your entries.

Repeat the steps for the BLN and WAMA systems.

Product Definition of Non-SAP Products

The SAP Solution Manager does not recognize all non-SAP applications. Therefore, you can define non-SAP products yourself. For Toys Inc, we have to add the product WAMA—Warehouse Management system.

1 Call Transaction SMSY.

2 Select the **General Product Definitions** landscape component.

3 Select **Landscape Components · Create Object · Create Product**. A new dialog opens.

4 Enter the necessary data.

5 Save your entries.

6 You can set your product as **Active** or **Inactive.** To define your system landscape, you can only use active products. In order to define a product as **Active**, you must at least define one product version. The system uses this data in the system settings, where you can show and hide products. Inactive products are removed from all selection menus as a product for selection throughout the SAP Solution Manager.

7 Save your entries.

8 The system shows the new product in the left-hand side of the screen as shown in Figure 4.6.

Setting RFC Connections in the Satellite Systems

Functioning RFC connections in the satellite systems are the prerequisite for monitoring system components. RFC connections can only be generated for ABAP-based main instances. Before you generate RFC connections, you must meet the following requirements:

▶ You are authorized to log on to the destination system and to create a user there. You are authorized to create RFC connections in the local system and in the destination system.

▶ The satellite systems are accessible.

▶ The message-servers are accessible on the **General Information** tab in Transaction SMSY with the reference and system number supplied.

▶ The following conditions are necessary to generate RFC connections if you use routers in your network, or if your network for generating an RFC connection requires the Distributed Name Service (DNS) Name:

 ▶ You have created the message server of the satellite system in the system landscape as a host and have supplied routing information for this host.

 ▶ When creating the corresponding system, you have specified this host as a message server.

 ▶ The system for which you want to generate RFC connections is not marked as **planned.**

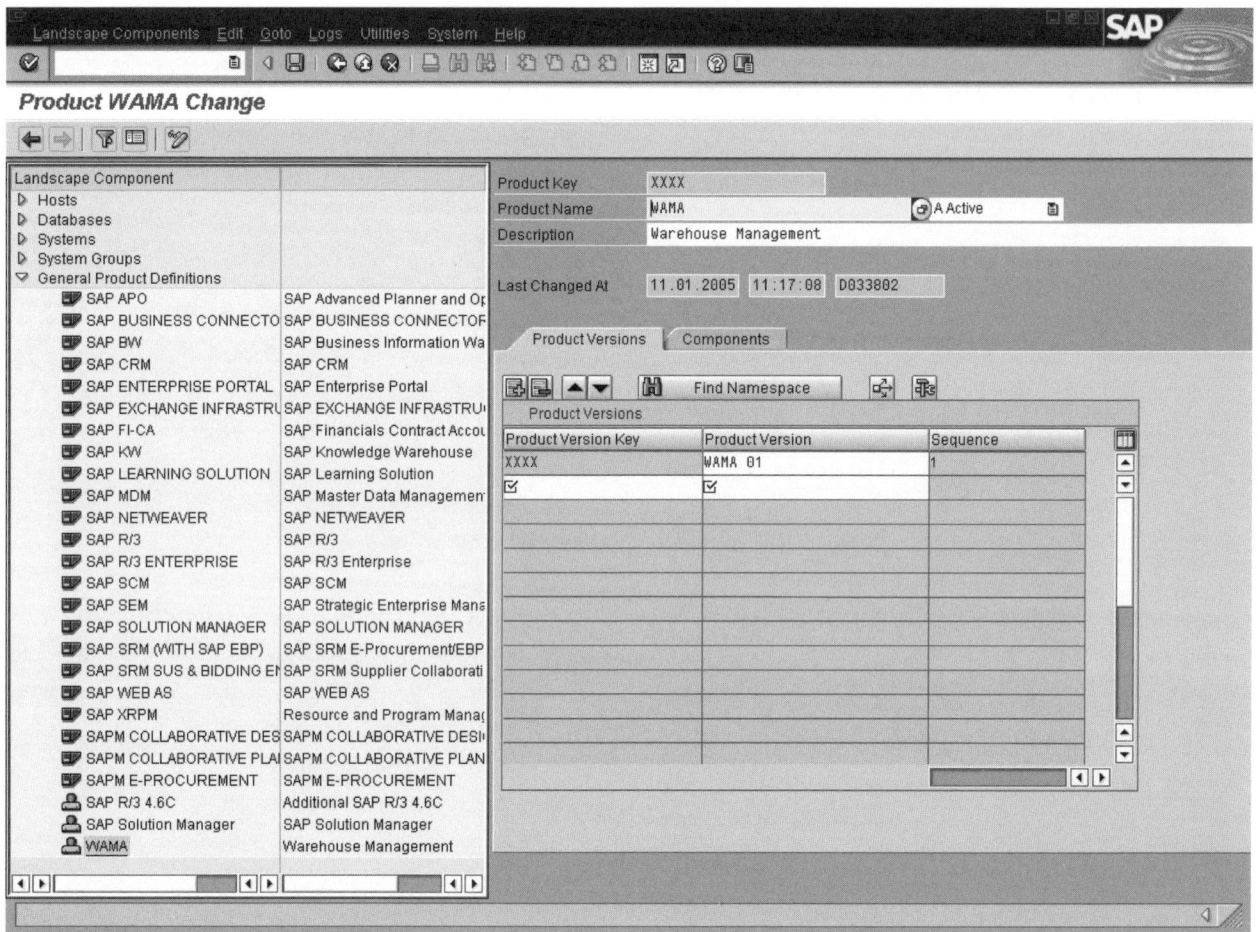

Figure 4.6   General Product Definitions

The following steps are necessary when generating RFC connections:

1   Call Transaction SMSY.

2   In the left-hand side of your display, select the ABAP-based main instance for which you want to generate RFC connections.

3   Change to the change mode.

4   Select a client from the **Clients** tab.

5   Click on **Generate RFC Destinations**.

6   Select the type or types of RFC connections in the following dialog.

When possible, we recommend that you select the trusted system as the RFC connection type for SAP Solution Manager. That enables you to avoid having to log on again each time you access a different component system when working with SAP Solution Manager. At the bottom of the screen, the system

shows you the details of the RFC connection to be generated.

7   Specify, where necessary, a server group for load distribution in the **RFC Destination Attributes** group box.

8   If merely providing a message server is not sufficient in your network to create an RFC connection, or, if you use routers in your network, do the following:

 ▸ Click on the **Routing Information** button in the **RFC Destination Attributes** group box.

 ▸ The following dialog displays data about the message server. If you have not yet created the system message server as a host, this host will automatically be created and will be displayed on the left under **Landscape Component** after Transaction SMSY has been restarted.

 ▸ Enter the IP address as necessary.

▶ Enter the routing information for the Solution Manager → Router → Host direction.

▶ Enter the routing information for the host → Router → Solution Manager direction.

▶ Save your entries.

9   Remote-read is preset for the system data as SAP Solution Manager needs current system data in order to read data on imported support packages for example. We recommend that you do not remove the check mark in the **Actions after Generation** group box.

10 Click on **Generate RFC Destinations**.

11 You will access several logon screens of the shared systems, according to the connection types selected.

12 Log onto the respective systems.

If generation errors occur, proceed as follows:

1   Note details from the message long texts in case of errors.

2   Troubleshoot the errors, if possible. You can enter the detailed view of the RFC connection in the **RFC Destination** transaction, by clicking the RFC connection in the **Generate RFC Destinations** dialog or by double-clicking the RFC connection in the **Clients** tab. From there, you can test the RFC connection and carry out any relevant changes. For more information, see the section "Removing Errors During RFC Generation."

3   If necessary, repeat the generation by cancelling the old RFC connection and then regenerating it.

4   Navigate backwards.

The system displays successfully generated RFC connections on the **Clients** tab. Repeat these steps for each system.

Service Data Control Center

The Service Data Control Center (SDCC) runs in the SAP Solution Manager system as well as in the satellite systems. It sends collected data to SAP Solution Manager. For example, weekly data can automatically be sent to SAP Solution Manager for the EarlyWatch Alert Service from all satellite systems. In order to ensure this, deter-

mine whether the latest version of SDCC is available in each system.

1   Call Transaction SDCC. It's possible that you could be asked in two dialog windows whether you would like to initiate a service preparation check or schedule the automatic session manager.

2   Select **Service Preparation Check**. You now go to RTCCTOOL. This is a tool that displays which SAP Notes must be implemented for the best possible data collection. Behind the SAP Notes, you will find information about which add-ons—ST-A/PI or ST-PI—still need to be imported.

3   Select **Automatic Session Manager** (ASM) in order to automate collection and transfer.

4   Select **Information · Version of program · SDCC** from the menu. You have now accessed the SDCC version information.

The next thing you have to do is set up the Automatic Session Manager.

The Automatic Session Manager (ASM) must be set up in the SDCC, in all satellite systems, and in the central SAP Solution Manager. Because you need ASM for the EarlyWatch Alert Service, it is recommended in any case.

The ASM is a periodical background job, which you can dispatch as follows:

1   Call Transaction SDCC.

2   Select **Settings · Autom. Sess. Manager** from the **Maintenance** menu. A new dialog opens.

3   Check the **You can activate the report associated with this job here** field.

4   Select the symbol beside the **Customizing** field. Another dialog screen opens.

5   Schedule the ASM. We recommend that you start the job during a period of low system load.

6   Save your entries.

In order to send monitoring data to SAP Solution Manager and to SAP, check whether the following RFC connections are maintained in SAP Solution Manager in SDCC:

1   Call Transaction SDCC in SAP Solution Manager.

2   Select **Remote environment · Default target system** from the **Maintenance** menu. A new dialog opens.

3   Assign the following three RFC connections:

Area	RFC connection
SAP service systems	SAPOSS
SAP Solution Manager system	NONE
Default target system for dynamic sessions	SAPOSS

Table 4.6   RFC Connections in SAP Solution Manager in SDCC

4. Save your entries.

An RFC connection is necessary to send data from the satellite system to SAP Solution Manager. RFC connections are also maintained via the SDCC:

1   Call Transaction SDCC in the satellite system.

2   Select **Remote environment · Default target system** from the **Maintenance** menu. A new dialog opens.

3   Assign the following three RFC connections:

Area	RFC connection
SAP service systems	SAPOSS
SAP Solution Manager system	RFC connection to the Solution Manager with an RFC User (e.g., user SOLMAN_RFC)
Default target system for dynamic sessions	SAPOSS

Table 4.7   RFC Connections in SAP Solution Manager in SDCC

4   Save your entries.

4.4   Solution Landscapes in SAP Solution Manager

The first step in setting up the system monitoring in SAP Solution Manager is to create an active solution. This section describes the creation of a solution landscape in SAP Solution Manager 3.1. As we mentioned in Chapter 1, there are differences between the interface display and navigation in releases 2.1, 2.2, and 3.2.

Overview of Active Solutions

In the SAP Solution Manager environment, a solution landscape is also abbreviated as "solution." In the Solution_Manager transaction entry screen, you get an overview of all the active solutions. There is a status overview for every solution. The example in Figure 4.7 gives you a status overview of the System Monitoring active solution.

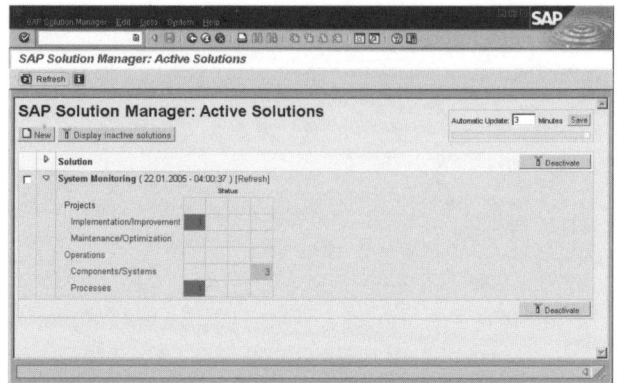

Figure 4.7   SAP Solution Manager 3.1—Active Solutions—Status Overview

You can get a status overview in the following areas:

▶ **Implementation/Improvement**
This gives you direct access to the implementation object overview.

▶ **Maintenance/Optimization**
You have direct access to the setup area for the Project Scoping and Issue Tracking solution.

▶ **Operations**
From here you can schedule SAP services or organize services to be provided by SAP.

▶ **Components/Systems**
Here you gain a complete overview of the system monitoring of your system components. From this description, you will be able to recognize the number of objects for which an alarm exists (red or yellow), as well as the number of objects that don't contain any problems (green). You'll get a graphic overview of the system monitoring of the solution.

▶ **Processes**
As is the case in **Components/System**, you will get preliminary status information about business process monitoring with regard to the number of objects for which an alarm was triggered.

The status shows the number of objects (projects, processes, or services) in red, yellow, or green. Red traffic lights indicate that serious errors have been detected, or alerts with a high-severity level have been issued. This means that the system operation is endangered. Yellow traffic lights indicate that the operating system is not under threat. Green traffic lights signify that a monitored value is in a permitted area.

Creating the "System Monitoring" Solution

Whether you want to combine all your satellite systems in one solution landscape or distribute them over several solutions is a matter of preference. It is certainly more advantageous that you differentiate among production systems, testing systems, and development systems, or create several solution landscapes for individual groups, for example.

1 Call Transaction Solution_Manager. An overview of the active solutions is displayed.

2 Click on the **New** button. A new dialog opens (see Figure 4.8).
Here you will see the legal requirements that are a prerequisite to access the SAP Service Marketplace.

3 Enter a name for the solution landscape in the **Solution Description** field. Select a name for the solution landscape, which signifies which landscape it belongs to. In our example, it is called *System Monitoring*.

4 Enter the customer number, the installation number, and the database ID into the corresponding fields. The solution landscape contains the customer number and the installation number of the central administration system of the system landscape, if it exists.

This is a requirement for managing access to the system landscape.

5 Set an update interval for the graphic monitoring interface.

6 Save the settings by clicking on the **OK** button.

7 The new solution is created and the **Operations Setup** screen is displayed. The newly created solution is empty at first. You must now assign the systems to be monitored and administered to the solution.

Deactivating an Active Solution

You can deactivate solution landscapes that are no longer used. You cannot display any services in a deactivated solution and you cannot make any changes.

1 Call Transaction Solution_Manager.

2 Mark the solution landscape by setting a flag in the white left checkbox beside the solution description.

3 Click on the **Deactivate** button.

4 If you would like to view all deactivated solution landscapes, click on the **Display inactive solutions** button. You will see all deactivated solutions in a new dialog. You can reactivate deactivated solutions at any time by clicking on the **Activate** button.

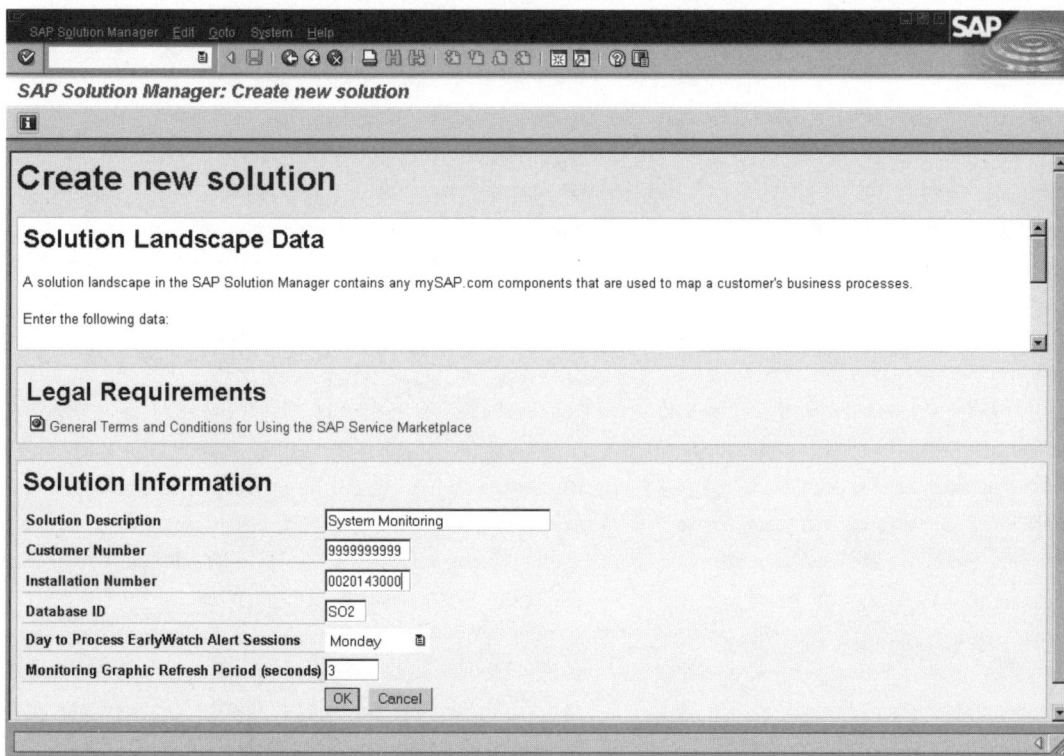

Figure 4.8 Creating a New Solution

4.5 Configuring the "System Monitoring" Solution

In the next step, the *System Monitoring* solution is assigned to the systems that are incorporated into the monitoring system. Before this, however, we must describe the structure of the main SAP Solution Manager screen.

The Basic Structure of the Main Screen of a Solution Landscape

The main screen of an active solution in SAP Solution Manager is divided into three areas: **Implementation**, **Operations Setup**, and **Operations sections.** Figure 4.9 illustrates the main screen.

The **Operations Setup** and **Operations areas are relevant for system monitoring.** Therefore, we will now focus on them in our description and not on the implementation area.

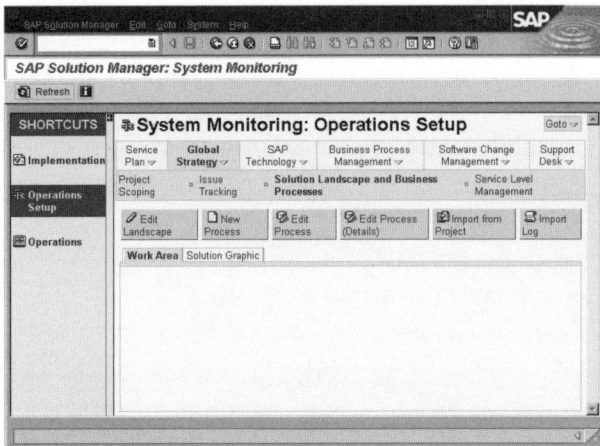

Figure 4.9 SAP Solution Manager 3.1—Main Screen

▶ **Operations Setup**

The **Operations Setup** area enables you to set and configure functionalities, which you can use to operate your system landscape. Various service categories are provided, which can, in turn, be structured into different sub-sections. Each of these sub-sections may or may not have a work area.

The following sections provide you with an overview and a description of the individual service categories and their sub-sections:

Service category	Sub-sections/function
Service plan	Using SAP services Access to SAP Service Channel Overview of certifications
Global strategy	Project overview Message overview Creating system landscapes and business processes Setting service level reporting
SAP Technology	Setting up system monitoring Setting up system management
Business Process Management	Setting up Business Process Management
Software Change Management	Using the Software Change Management Services
Support Desk	Integrating message processing for your own internal support organization and enhanced SAP remote support

Table 4.8 Service Categories of SAP Solution Manager 3.1

The relevant Best Practices documents are available for all service categories and their sub-sections according to their functionality.

▶ **Operations**

By selecting **Operations**, you use the functionalities that you have previously set up in the **Operations Setup** area.

Integrating the Systems in System Monitoring

After creating the solution landscape, you should assign the systems to it. This means that the only systems that will be integrated into the system monitoring will be those already created in SMSY. You can also incorporate other systems into the solution landscape at a later stage.

In the Toys Inc. example, the BLA, BLN, and WAMA systems are assigned to the active *System Monitoring* solution:

1 Select Operations Setup.

2 Select **Global Strategy · Solution Landscape and Business Processes · Edit Landscape.**

3 On the left of the screen, select **System groups · Solution Landscapes-Operation · System Monitoring.** On the right of the screen, you'll get an overview of all systems connected to the SAP Solution Manager. In the **Assigned** column, check the systems that are

to be assigned to this solution landscape. Figure 4.10 shows the system classification in the *System Monitoring* solution landscape:

▶ BLA application component: SAP APO 3.1

▶ BLN application component: SAP R/3

▶ WAMA application component: WAMA 01

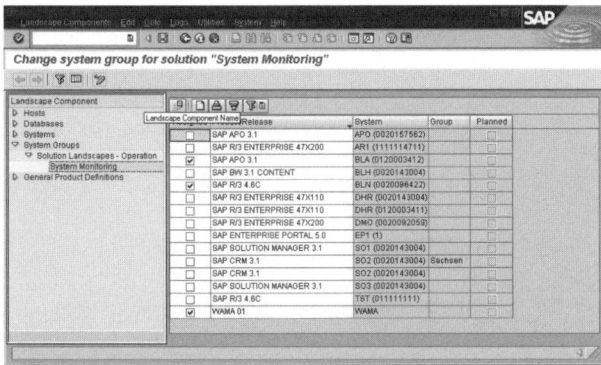

Figure 4.10 Assigning Systems to the System Monitoring Solution Landscape

4 Save your entries.

5 Click on **Back** to return to the operation mode of SAP Solution Manager.

The systems are displayed in SAP Solution Manager for operation. The newly installed systems now appear in the **SAP Technology** solution graphic.

Assigning RFC Connections for System Monitoring

For security reasons, two RFC connections are created to monitor the satellite systems, as there are two main differences in the requirements for the monitoring and monitored systems.

▶ **RFC destination for data collection**

Data collection methods are active in the monitored system, which store monitor attributes in the shared memory. The monitoring system reads out these values through an RFC call with a specific user name. In the system being monitored, this user is merely an observer who has to log on for each query. For this destination, you should use the CSMREG user, which is permitted to call only certain function modules.

▶ **RFC destination for analysis**

If a data collection method triggers an alarm, you can start an analysis method in the monitoring monitor for the monitoring attribute. You can make changes in the system being monitored, which require further authorizations. Use a dialog user to implement these changes.

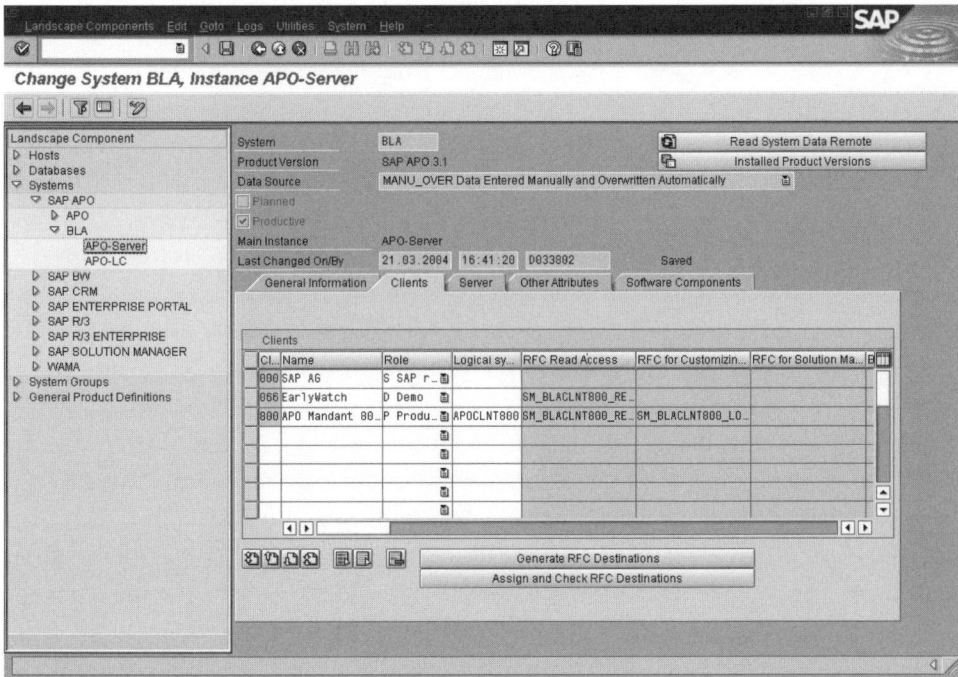

Figure 4.11 Assigning and Checking RFC Destinations

You can assign RFC connections for central system monitoring in the operation mode of your solution landscape in SAP Solution Manager:

1 Select **Operations Setup**.

2 Select **Global Strategy · Solution Landscape and Business Processes · Edit Landscape**.

3 Select **Landscape Component · Systems · <Application component> · <System>**.

4 Select the corresponding hardware components. You will find information on the hardware on the right-hand side of the screen.

5 Select the **Clients** tab as shown in Figure 4.11.

6 Select the client line that should be assigned to the RFC connections.

7 Click on the **Assign and Check RFC Destinations button.** A new dialog opens.

8 Select the **Assign RFC Dest. for System Monitoring** field as shown in Figure 4.12. You only need to use this command for one client per system.

9 Save your entries.

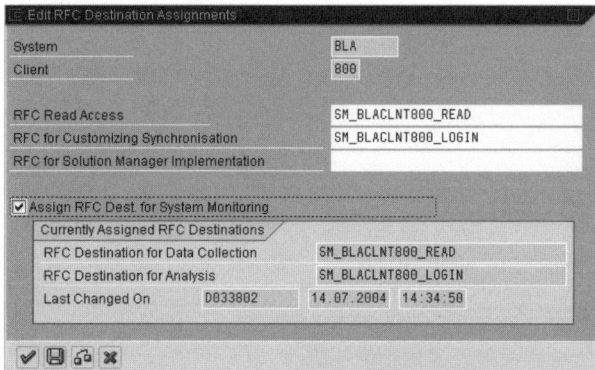

Figure 4.12 Assigning RFC Destinations for System Monitoring

The required RFC Destinations are assigned to a system. All RFC Destination data for the system is entered into central system monitoring. You can find an overview of the monitored remote systems in Transaction RZ21 (**Technical Infrastructure · Display Topology** on the **Monitored remote SAP system** tab.)

EarlyWatch Alert (EWA)
The EarlyWatch Alert (EWA) is a monitoring tool that monitors the administrative areas of SAP components and provides you—as system administrators—with updates on the performance and stability of the solution

landscape. The EWA runs automatically once a week. You can generate a report for each EWA run. The report contains information on the system status, performance, system configuration, system operation, system administration, and other items.

The following sections explain how you can generate and view the EWA report:

1 Select **Operations on the left side of the screen**.

2 Select **SAP Technology · Monitoring · Work Area**. You will get an overview of EarlyWatch Services for all SAP systems. From here, you can generate the report as an HTML document or as an MS Word document.

▶ **HTML document**
   1. Select a link to an EWA service.
   2. Select the report type. The report is generated.

▶ **Word document**
   1. Select the **Create Word Report** symbol in the **Activities** column.
   2. Select the report type. The report is generated.

4.6 Setting Up Active System Monitoring

In this section, we will implement the system monitoring requirements. You will learn how to set up system monitoring. The monitoring concept created for Toys Inc. in Chapter 3 will form the basis for this implementation. You should note that the setup and maintenance of monitoring objects in SAP Solution Manager 3.1 will only be described using a few monitoring objects that are contained in the active monitoring process. Furthermore, a complete description of the implementation of the monitoring concept doesn't need to be repeated for each of the three systems, as the configuration steps are the same each time. The following section also discusses how the setup procedure affects other systems. We advise you to carry out the following steps in the order described.

Basic Information on the Structure of the "System Monitoring Setup" Service
Let's first look at the structure of the screen for the Setup System Monitoring service. You must be in the active solution in which you want to set up system monitoring. Take the following steps to get there:

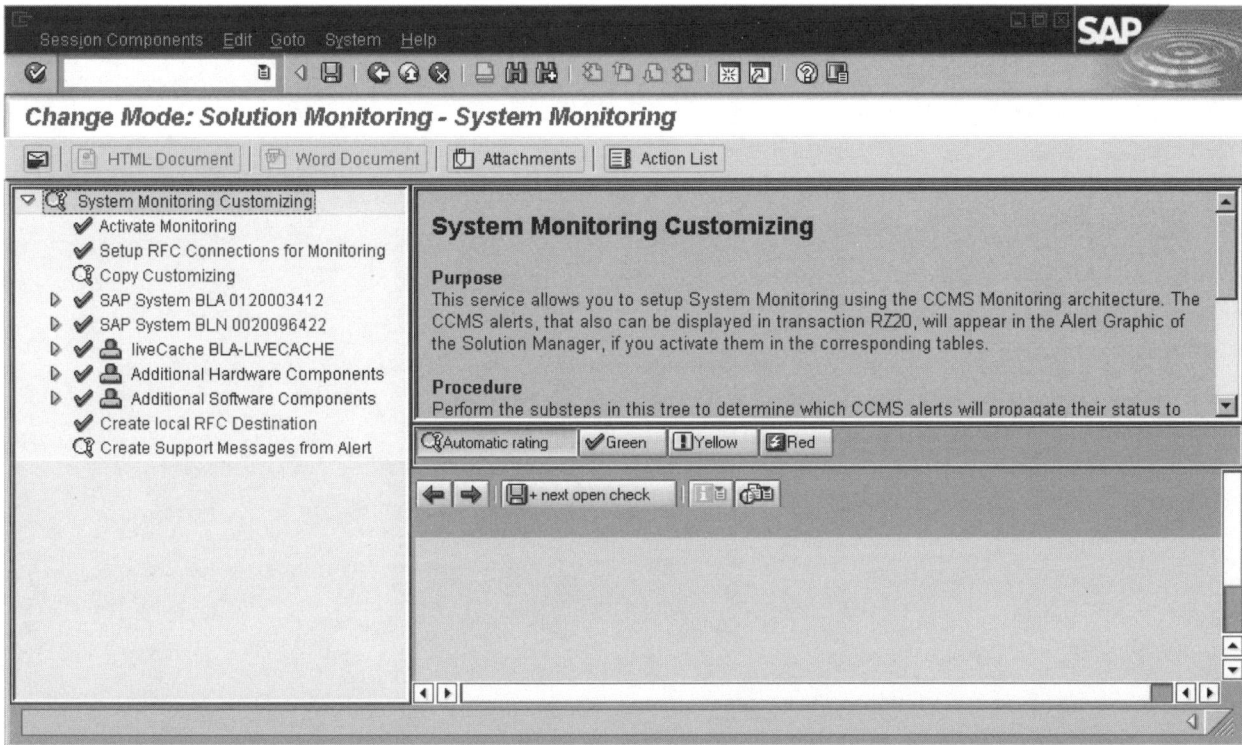

Figure 4.13 System Monitoring Setup Service

1 Select **Operations Setup**.

2 Select **SAP Technology · Monitoring · Setup System Monitoring** in the right part of the screen. You are now in the system monitoring configuration service, as illustrated in Figure 4.13.

The screen is divided into three areas.

In the left pane of the screen, you'll see a tree structure that you will use to set up system monitoring. It is divided into:

▶ General checks
    ▶ Monitoring activation
    ▶ Setup RFC Connections for monitoring
    ▶ Copy Customizing
▶ System-specific subchecks
    ▶ Setup Monitoring for SAP Systems
    ▶ User-defined alerts
▶ Additional hardware components (optional)
▶ Additional software components (optional)

The upper right-hand pane of the screen gives you a description and background information on whichever check you are in.

In the bottom left-hand pane, you can see the tables that you maintain for each corresponding check. This is where you can enter threshold value definitions for the monitoring objects.

Activating System Monitoring for SAP Systems

Upon activation, you will receive predefined standard monitoring objects which you can use as a basis for the active system monitoring setup. In order to activate, proceed as follows:

1 You are in your solution landscape in the *System Monitoring Setup* service.

2 Select the **Activate Monitoring** check on the left-hand side of the screen. To the right of the screen, you'll see a list of SAP systems which, in this solution landscape, you can include in system monitoring, as shown in Figure 4.14.

3 In the **Active** column, check the systems to be included in monitoring.

4 Save your entries. A check is created for every activated system. You will recognize the check from the sequence of characters: **SAP System <SID> <Installation number>**.

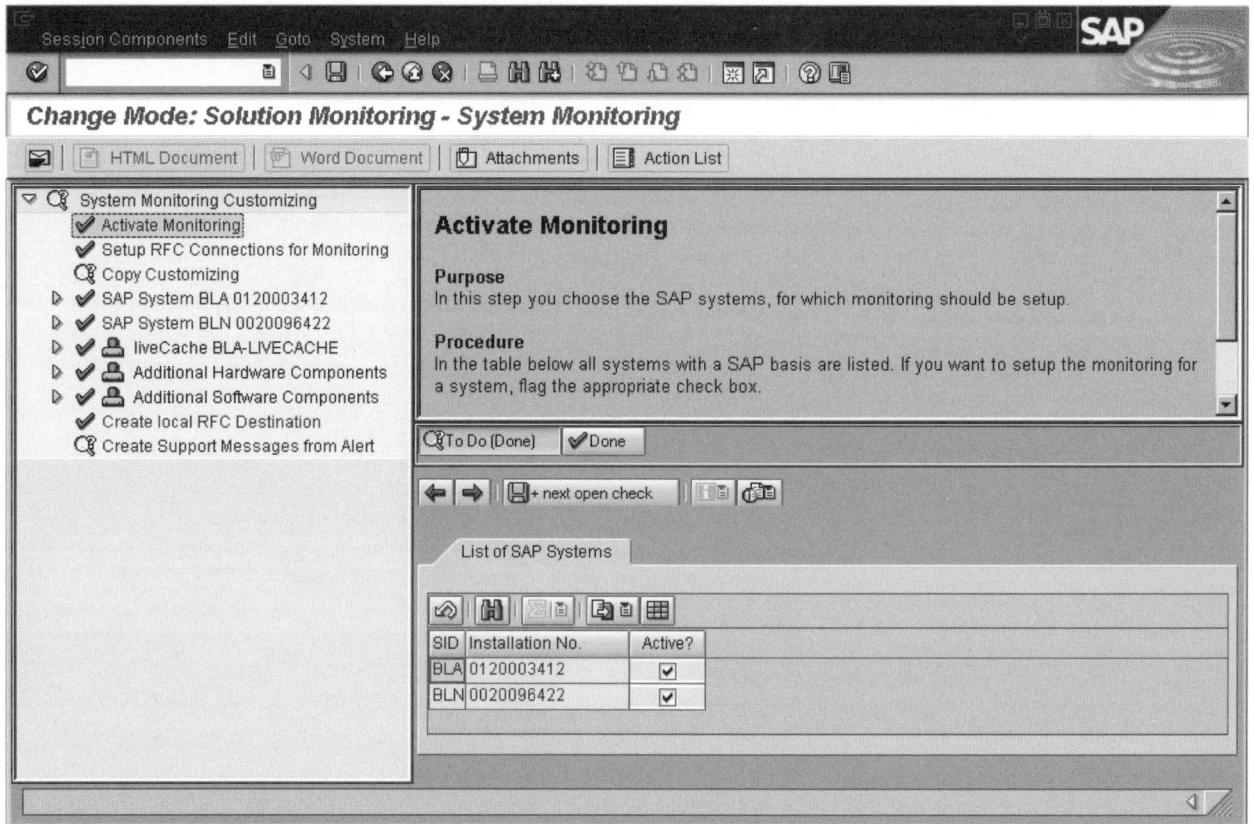

Figure 4.14   System Monitoring Service—Activate Monitoring

RFC Connections for System Monitoring

Two RFC connections are necessary for system monitoring: one for data collection and one for analysis. In the section "Assigning RFC Connections for System Monitoring", we already described how you can assign RFC connections. If you follow this step, a green check mark automatically appears in the **Status** column, as you can see in Figure 4.15. In this figure, the connections for data collection and analysis for the BLN and BLA systems have been successfully created.

If the RFC connections are not recognized or another problem occurs, the status is set to red. Follow the instructions in the upper right-hand corner of the screen to solve the problem. If necessary, delete the connections set in Transaction SM59 to regenerate them.

Setting Up System Monitoring for SAP Components

System monitoring for SAP components is set up under the system-specific sub-checks. These sub-checks refer to the individual SAP systems contained in the solution landscape for which the system monitoring was activated. According to the request, you can use predefined standard monitoring objects or individual user-defined objects. Please note that the monitoring objects in the CCMS must be accessible. Otherwise, they will not function in SAP Solution Manager.

In the Toys Inc. example, certain alerts can be integrated as we have already explained.

First, we have to set up the monitoring of the operating system. According to the Toys Inc. monitoring concept file systems, CPUs, storage use, OS Collector, and Swap Space are monitored. Activate the monitoring objects for the operating system:

1   Go to the *System Monitoring Setup* service.

2   Select **System Monitoring Customizing · SAP System <SID> <Installation number> · Server <Hostname> · Setup Monitoring for Server <Hostname>**. Maintain the standard monitoring objects CPU, Paging, OS Collector, and their threshold values.

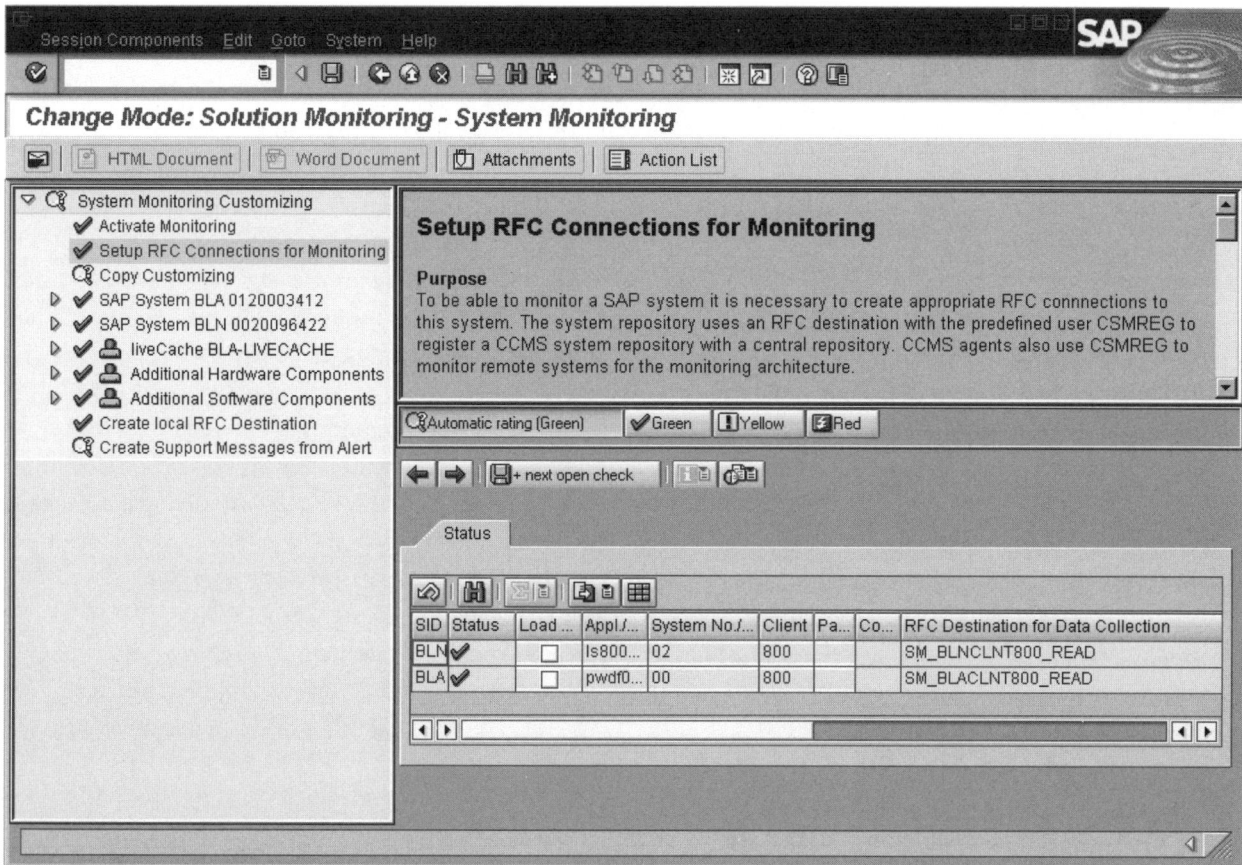

Figure 4.15 RFC Connections for System Monitoring

3 Save your entries.

4 Select **System Monitoring Customizing · SAP System <SID> <Installation number> · Server <Hostname> · User Defined Alerts for <Hostname>** to set up the swap space and the file systems for monitoring.

5 Select the monitoring object in the selection field in the **Alert Name** column and select the **Transfer** button.

6 Save your entries.

Next, we must set up instance availability and system availability monitoring.

The prerequisite for checking the instance and system availability is the installation of the CCMSPING agent. You can install and configure this agent on any host. By using the agent, we can centrally control the availability of systems.

When the agent is being used, carry out the following activities to set up instance-availability monitoring in SAP Solution Manager:

1 Go to the *System Monitoring Setup* service.

2 Select **System Monitoring Customizing · SAP System <SID> <Installation number> · SAP Application Server <Hostname_SID_Systemnumber> · Instance Availability of <Hostname_SID_Systemnumber>**.

3 Activate the **Instance Status** alert.

4 Save your entries.

System availability should be superordinate to all instances. It is therefore advisable to activate system availability in **System Monitoring Customizing · SAP System <SID> <Installation number> · User Defined Alerts <SID> <Installation number>**.

The next step is setting up system performance monitoring. There is a range of standard monitoring objects available for system performance.

1 You are now in the *System Monitoring Setup* service.
2 Select **System Monitoring Customizing · SAP System <SID> <Installation number> · SAP Application Server <Hostname_SID_System number> · Performance Alerts of <Hostname_SID_System number>**. Activate the monitoring objects according to the monitoring concept target.
3 Save your entries.
4 If the monitoring objects are not set as standard in SAP Solution Manager, use the **System Monitoring Customizing · SAP System <SID> <Installation number> · SAP Application Server <Hostname_SID_System number> · User Defined Alerts of <Hostname_SID_System number>** check. At this point, enter the missing monitoring objects.
5 Save your entries.

After that, database monitoring must be set up. You can set criteria to monitor the database performance as well as administrative monitoring objects as follows:

1 You are now in the *System Monitoring Setup* service.
2 Select **System Monitoring Customizing · SAP System <SID> <Installation number> · Database <SID>-DATABASE**. Activate the monitoring objects in the underlying checks according to the specifications of your monitoring concept.
3 Save your entries.
4 If the monitoring concept does not set monitoring objects as standard in SAP Solution Manager, use the **System Monitoring Customizing · SAP System <SID> <Installationsnummer> · Database <SID>-DATABASE · User Defined Alerts for <SID>-DATABASE** check. Enter the missing alerts.
5 Save your entries.

Copying System Monitoring Configuration Settings

The system monitoring settings that you have set for an SAP component can be transferred to other SAP components too. To do this, copy the monitoring object settings. You can do this for the database instance, the R/3 system, the server, and the database. Note that the database copy mechanism functions only with similar database types.

1 You are now in the *System Monitoring Setup* service.
2 Select **System Monitoring Customizing · Copy Customizing**.
3 Select from the context if you want to copy the alert settings to the instance, the R/3 system, the server, or the database.
4 Select the source and destination systems.
5 Click on the **Copy** button and save the entries to start the copying mechanism. The settings conform to the corresponding target component.

Setting up System Monitoring for Additional SAP Components—liveCache

Toys Inc. uses the SAP APO solution. Configuration steps for general system monitoring of SAP components have already been described earlier in this book. LiveCache Monitoring setup, another component in SAP APO, will be carried out in this section.

Minimum requirements for using the LiveCache alert monitor are the following Basis-Support-Package releases:

▶ SAP Basis 4.6C: SP40
▶ SAP Basis 4.6D: SP29
▶ SAP Basis 6.10: SP28
▶ SAP Basis 6.20: SP16

Proceed as follows:

1 You are now in the *System Monitoring Setup* service.
2 Select **System Monitoring Customizing · liveCache <SID>-liveCache**.
3 Select the APO system in which the liveCache is active, and the related CCMS context using the **F4** help.
4 Save your entries.
5 Select **System Monitoring Customizing · liveCache <SID>-liveCache · Errors/Administrating of <SID>-liveCache**. Activate the corresponding monitoring objects according to the monitoring concept.
6 Save your entries.
7 Select **System Monitoring Customizing · liveCache <SID>-liveCache · Performance/Availability of <SID>-liveCache**. Activate the corresponding monitoring objects according to the monitoring concept.
8 Save your entries.

9   If the monitoring concept does not set certain monitoring objects as standard in SAP Solution Manager, use the **System Monitoring Customizing · Monitoring Customizing · liveCache <SID>-liveCache · User Defined Alerts for <SID>-liveCache** check. Enter the missing objects.

10 Save your entries.

Setting Up System Monitoring for Additional Hardware Components

In addition to SAP system hardware, the hardware of non-SAP systems can also be monitored. That requires that the CCMS monitoring objects are recognized in the central monitoring system. This means that data about operating system resources of non-SAP components can be collected, if, as described in Chapter 3, the SAP-CCMSR and SAPOSCOL agents are installed.

In the Toys Inc. example, WAMA, the non-SAP application, runs on its own host. This host's operating system data should be monitored according to the monitoring concept.

1   You are now in the *System Monitoring Setup* service.

2   Select **System Monitoring Customizing · Additional Hardware Components**.

3   Select the hardware to be monitored. Flag the **To monitor** column to activate monitoring.

4   Save your entries. Depending on the selection, further checks will be carried out on the relevant server.

5   Select **System Monitoring Customizing · Additional Hardware Components · Hardware Component Server <hostname>**. Select the CCMS context for the server.

6   Save your entries.

7   Select **System Monitoring Customizing · Additional Hardware Components · Hardware Component Server <hostname> · Setup monitoring for Server <SID>**. Activate the corresponding monitoring objects according to the monitoring concept.

8   Save your entries.

9   If the monitoring concept does not set certain monitoring objects as standard in SAP Solution Manager, use the **System Monitoring Customizing · Monitoring Customizing · Additional Hardware Components · Hardware Component Server <hostname> · User Defined Alerts for <hostname>** check. Enter the missing objects.

10 Save your entries.

System Monitoring Setup for Additional Software Components

As is the case when monitoring additional hardware components, applications outside the SAP world in SAP Solution Manager can be monitored as well. A prerequisite for this is also that monitoring objects must be recognized in the CCMS:

1   You are now in the *System Monitoring Setup* service.

2   Select **System Monitoring Customizing · Additional Software Components**.

3   At the bottom right part of the screen, select **None-SAP-Application** in the **Type** column. In the **Name** column, select the component from the selection help to be monitored.
    Figure 4.16 shows the assignment of the WAMA non-SAP component at Toys Inc.

4   Save your entries. Depending on the selection, other checks will be created for each application.

5   Select **System Monitoring Customizing · Additional Software Components · Specify Central Monitoring System**.

6   From the selection help, select the monitoring system in which the monitoring objects are recognized by the CCMS. This is usually the central monitoring system.

7   Save your entries.

8   Select **System Monitoring Customizing · Additional Software Components · Alert Customizing of NON-SAP-APPLICATION**. Activate the monitoring objects.

9   Save your entries.

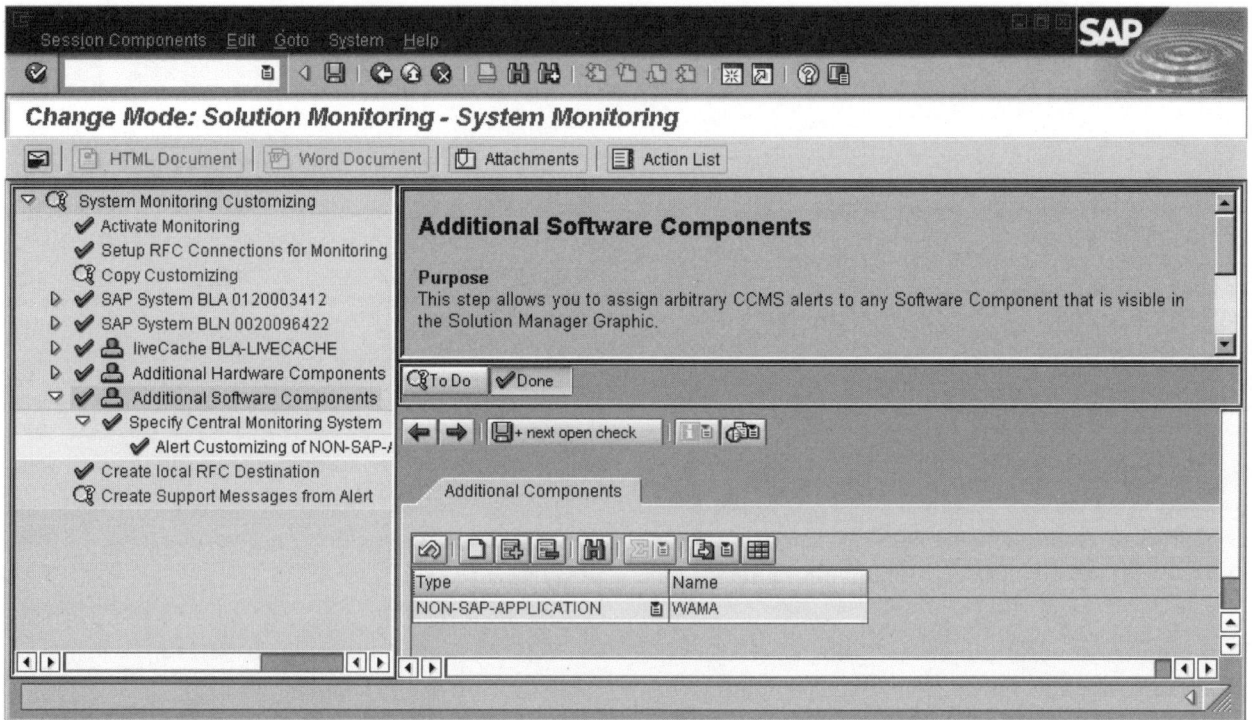

Figure 4.16   Defining Additional Software Components in the Monitoring System

4.7   The SAP Solution Manager Alert Monitor

Alerts are a central element in monitoring IT landscapes as they provide fast and reliable reports or warnings. These alerts are displayed in the Alert Monitor.

Principles of the Alert Monitor

Before we provide a graphical overview of the system components and their monitoring objects and alerts in SAP Solution Manager, you will first receive some general information on the Alert Monitor. The Alert Monitor concept comes from the CCMS world and can similarly be transferred to the SAP Solution Manager. Both in CCMS (via Transaction RZ20) and in SAP Solution Manager, you can view alerts from the various monitoring objects. However, the display of both areas is entirely different. From a functional view, there is no difference. The SAP Solution Manager reverts to the monitoring architecture of the CCMS.

We distinguish between two different views in the Alert Monitor. These are:

▶ **Open Alerts**

   Open Alerts show all problems that have not yet been analyzed by the system administrator. Addi-

tional details regarding some of the alerts are shown in the Alert Monitor. These details contain information on the current threshold value and the current value that has exceeded or fallen short of the threshold value and caused the alarm. You can get information on other alerts if you go directly to the monitored system.

Figure 4.17 shows open alerts for Instance PWDF0445_BLA_00 at Toys Inc. in SAP Solution Manager. For the *Load+Gen time* monitoring object, you can see two yellow alerts and one red alert. To analyze these alerts, simply click on the **[More]** field to see the system that is monitored.

▶ **Current Status**

   The **Current Status** view provides information on the latest reported data on the components. The color of the individual monitoring objects (red, yellow, or green) shows their status at that time and is independent of possible open alerts. It is possible for the dialog response time to have exceeded or fallen below the threshold value of a monitoring object. The result is a yellow or red alert in the current overview display. During the next data collection, the value is

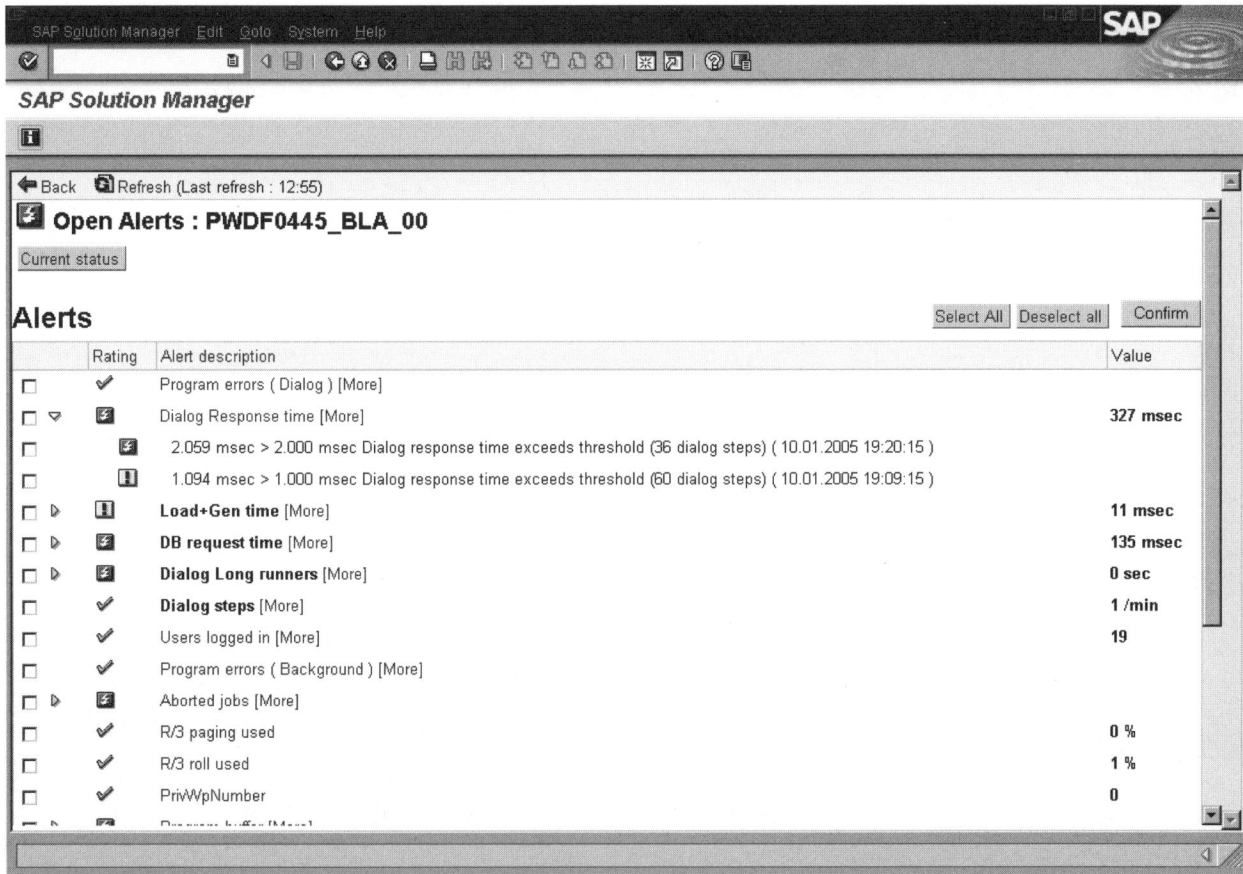

Figure 4.17 Alert Monitor in SAP Solution Manager: Open Alerts View

once again in the green area. The result is that the current status of the monitoring object changes back to green.

The Alert Monitor after the Setup Process for System Monitoring

After completing the setup for the monitoring objects and defining threshold values for each alert, you can see the result immediately after the next data collection in the graphic overview:

1 You are in the active solution.

2 Select **Operations**.

3 Select **SAP Technology · Monitoring · Solution graphics · Fullscreen**. You are now in the System Group Overview. In Figure 4.18, you can see the SAP APO, SAP R/3, and WAMA system components according to our example of system monitoring for Toys Inc.

Each system component contains at least one sub-component. In order to view details on the system components, select the respective components. The specified monitoring objects for the components with their values at that time appear.

Figure 4.19 shows the operation system alerts for the BLA system for the PWDF0445 host. To the right of the alerts, you can see the values. On the left-hand side in the **Rating** column, the current status of the last reported data is displayed in a color.

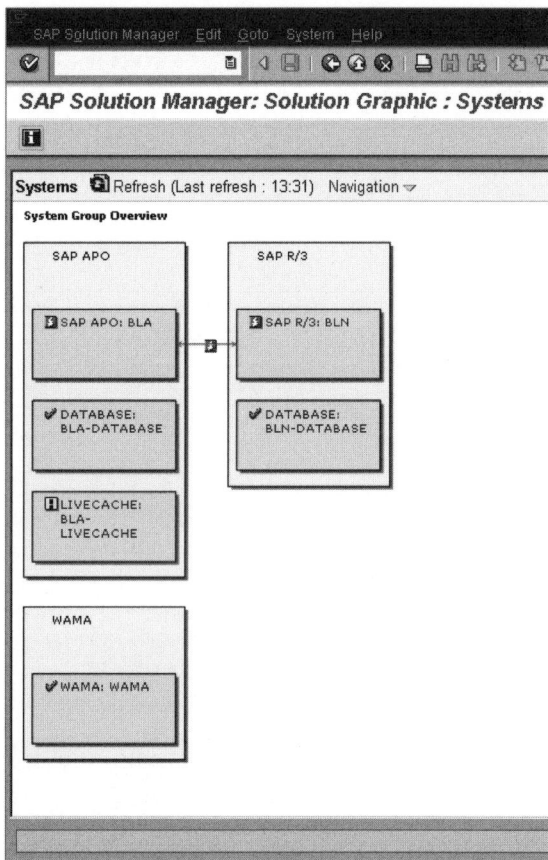

Figure 4.18 System Group Overview

Figure 4.19 HTML Graphic—Detailed Alert Display

4.8 Setting Up Manual System Monitoring

In addition to setting up system monitoring, which focuses on active, automatic monitoring of certain monitoring objects, you can set up manual system monitoring or system administration using another service in SAP So-

lution Manager. That means you can define administrative tasks that have to be implemented daily, weekly, monthly, or, as needed in the system. For some of these tasks, monitoring objects can, in turn, be defined in SAP Solution Manager. Outstanding tasks are then displayed in the graphical solution landscape; however, setup comes first. This is implemented as follows:

1 You are in your solution landscape.
2 Select **Operations Setup** in the left-hand pane.
3 Select **SAP Technology · Administration · Central System Administration.** You are now in the System Monitoring Setup (see Figure 4.20).
4 Define which SAP systems and SAP Internet middleware components should be administered under **Central System Administration · Choose Administration and Monitoring Workarea · SAP Systems Table.**
5 In addition to this, under **Central System Administration · Choose Administration and Monitoring Workarea · Administration and Monitoring Workarea, you can** select which view variant you would like to have on the system tasks. You can choose from the following three variants:
  ▶ **Entire**—This option gives you an overview of all system tasks.
  ▶ **Tasks Worklist**—This option gives you an overview of all open system tasks depending on the frequency of the task execution.
  ▶ **Daily Open**—This option gives you an overview of all the open tasks that are operated daily.
6 Save your entries.
7 You can modify the view variants under **Central System Administration · Tasks View Master.** For instance, you can display all open system tasks for this month in a view variant.
8 In **Central System Administration · Report Customizing (Tasks Log History),** you can determine for which systems you would like to create a log evaluation of past system monitoring. Select the systems you want to create a report for from the **Report Content for Tasks Log History** tab. The report will contain all entries that are in the **Tasks Log History** tab.

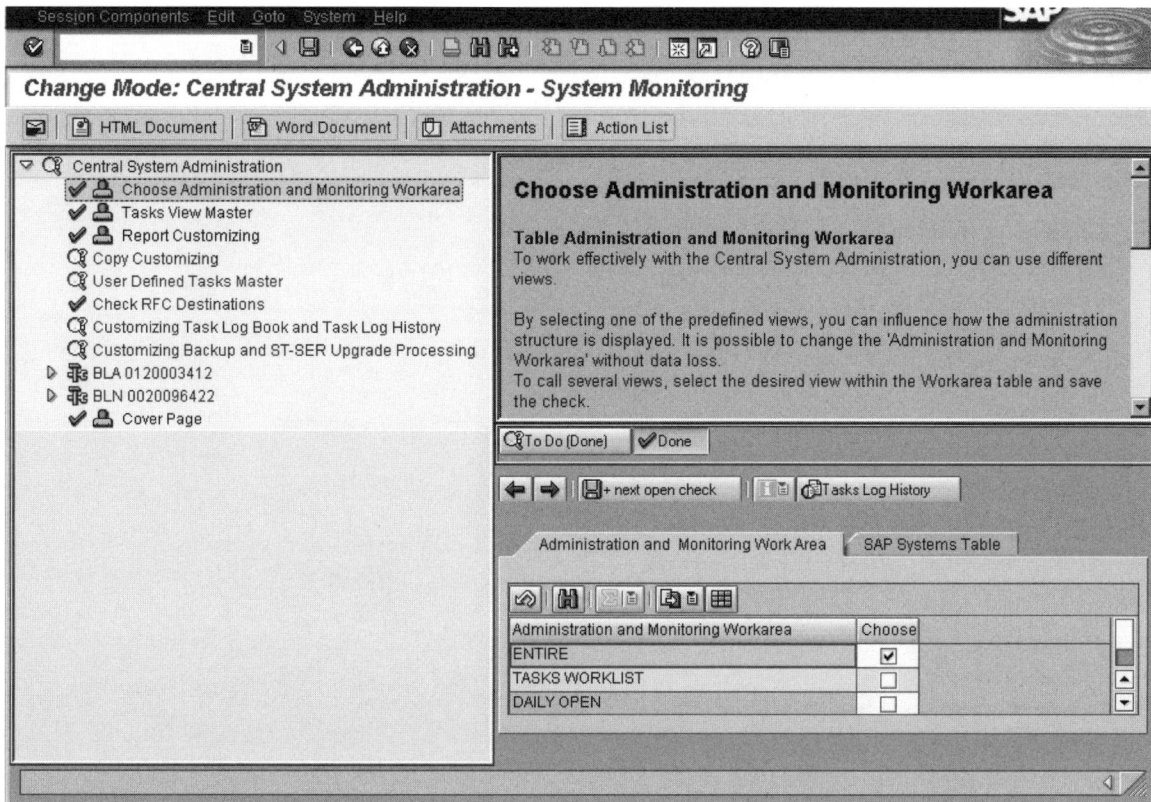

Figure 4.20 Service for Manual System Monitoring

9 You also can define the period of the log history that will appear in the report. To do this, use the **Define Content for Task Log History** tab.

10 Save your entries.

In the next step, define which system tasks have to be executed at what point in each system.

1 Select **Central System Administration · <System-ID Installation number>**. You can see three tabs on the right-hand side of the screen:

▶ **System Type**—Select the system type: Production System, Quality Assurance System, Development System, and Demo System.

▶ **Involved Component**—Select the relevant SAP components for this system. Additional system tasks must be set correspondingly for the component.

▶ **User Defined Tasks**—If you have defined individual system tasks in the **Central System Administration · User Defined Tasks Master** check, you

can select these in the **Task** selection field with the corresponding **Group**.

2 Save your entries.

Depending on the components selected, you will receive a range of sub-checks under **<System-ID Installation number>**. In our example, these are the following sub-checks for the BLA system (see Figure 4.21):

▶ General Basis Administration Tasks Group
▶ Database Administration Tasks Group
▶ Performance Monitoring Tasks Group
▶ mySAP SCM Administration
▶ User Defined Tasks Group

For each of these checks, a range of additional sub-checks is offered. Here, you can select which tasks should be included in your system administration (see Figure 4.22).

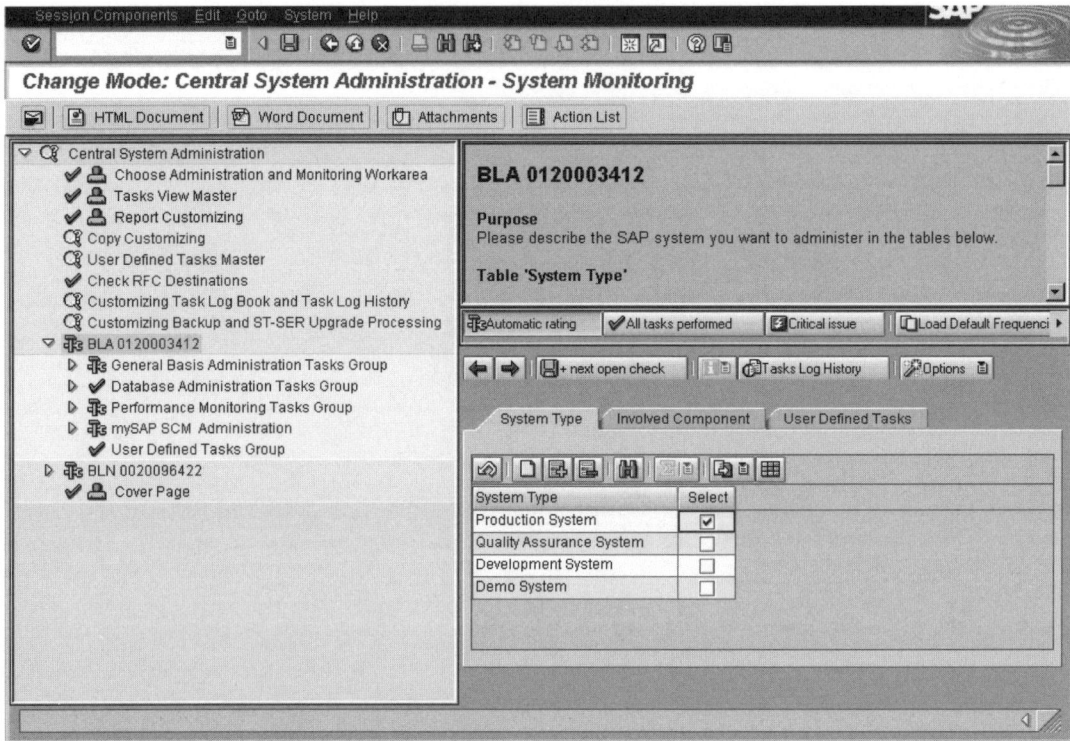

Figure 4.21   Defining System Tasks for Each System

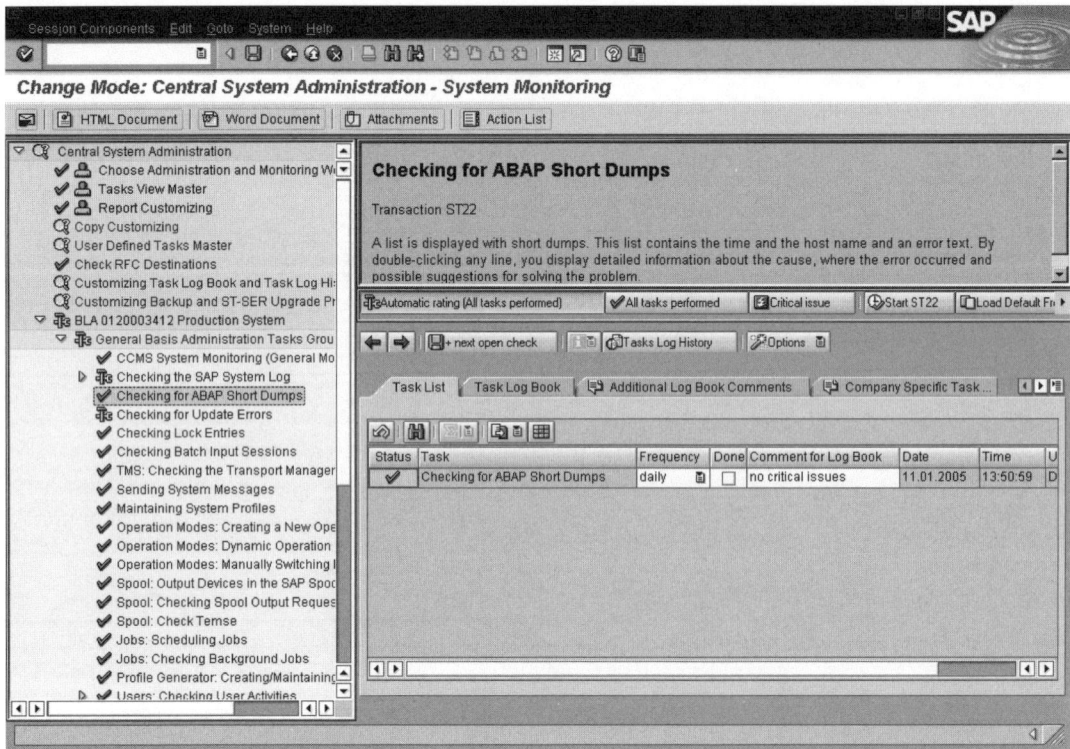

Figure 4.22   Selection of System Tasks per System and Functional Areas

Then set up system monitoring:

1 Proceed step by step through each individual check and verify whether this task must be executed in your system monitoring. On the right-hand side of the screen, you can see four tabs per system task:

▶ **Task List**

Select the frequency (daily, weekly, monthly, yearly, if necessary, not active) of the monitoring activity. You will use both of the other columns **Done and Comment for Log Book** in the monitoring process. Here, in the case of an alert, you can enter information on the alert as well as measures you have implemented to resolve the problem. However, for the implementation of the central system monitoring, this information and the troubleshooting measures are irrelevant.

▶ **Task Log Book**

This is where which user has carried out which system task and when that task was performed is logged.

▶ **Additional Log Book Comments**

This is where whoever has executed the task can store additional comments on monitoring. If, for instance, an escalation has to be started, it can be logged at this time.

▶ **Company Specific Task Description**

In this tab, you can set troubleshooting procedures, escalation procedures, and responsibilities, for example.

2 Save your entries.

After setting up central system monitoring, you will see the symbol instead of a green rating for each task you have defined. It means that a task was defined at this point. You will also find this symbol later in the graphical display of the system monitoring.

Graphical Display of the Central System Administration

After setting up the central administration, you can view the result in a graphical overview. The HTML graphic makes the system—in which the administrative tasks are stored—easily recognizable. The system tasks are displayed in accordance with the frequency of the monitoring.

1 You are in the active solution.

2 Select **Operations**.

3 Select **SAP Technology · Administration · Solution Graphic**. Select **Fullscreen.** You are now in the graphical overview display for system monitoring (see Figure 4.23).

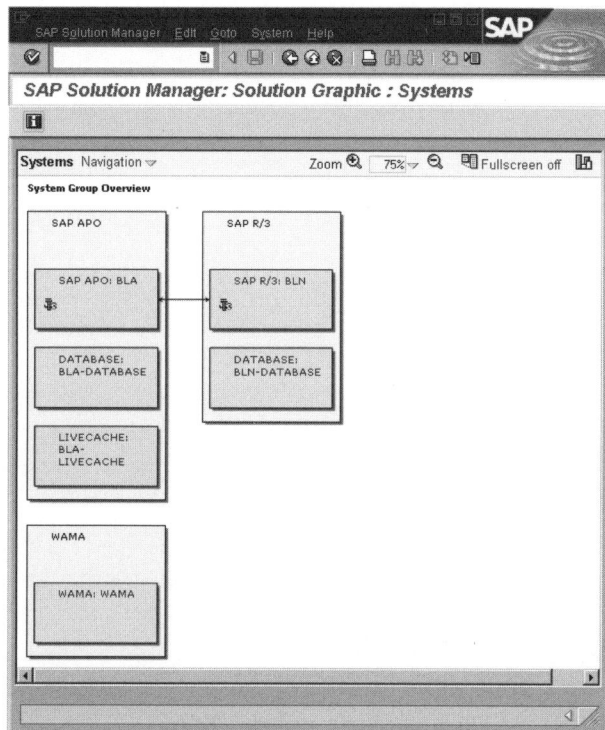

Figure 4.23 Central System Monitoring—HTML Solution Graphic

4 Select the symbol in each system. A new dialog opens in which the tasks are defined per system (see Figure 4.24).

5 Select a task. You are now in the central system administration service. Here you can go directly into the system to be monitored in order to execute the system task. Upon completing the task, confirm this completion and, if necessary, write a comment into the **Log Book.**

6 Save your entries. The symbol is replaced by a green rating. The task disappears from the task list of the graphical overview until the next necessary monitoring activity.

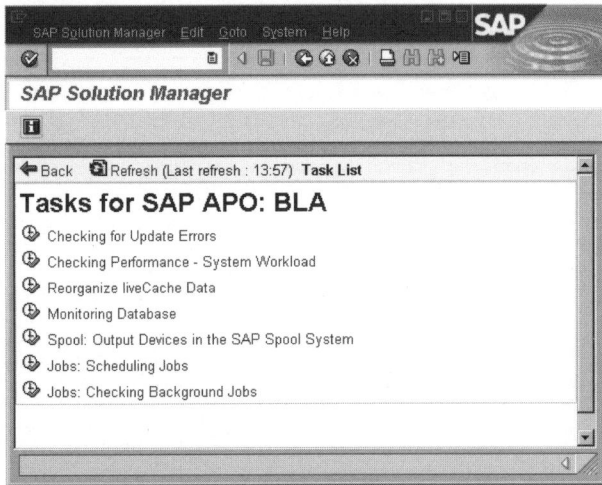

Figure 4.24 System Tasks for the APO System BLA

4.9 Autoreaction Methods

When you monitor a system landscape, the system administrator receives prompt notification of any problems that have occurred. Autoreaction methods such as email notifications, SMS, fax, or pager are a very helpful means of support here.

The method by which the system administrator receives information regarding a problem that has occurred depends on what influence the object to be monitored has on the running system operation. If, for example, a system breaks down, it is advisable that you notify the system administrator both via the monitoring team and an autoreaction method.

In the SAP Solution Manager system, autoreaction methods are defined via the CCMS monitoring architecture. Since SAP Basis Release 4.0, the CCMS monitoring architecture enables you to define autoreaction methods, which are automatically executed in case of an emergency.

Since SAP Basis Release 4.6A, the predefined autoreaction method—CCMS_OnAlert_E-mail—is supplied. This method automatically selects email, pager, or fax. Even if you are not already logged onto the Alert Monitor, you'll receive a message.

Since SAP Basis Release 6.10, central autoreaction methods can be defined in central monitoring. The autoreaction methods are then configured in the system in which the central monitoring is executed.

This chapter describes the technical implementation for the email autoreaction method. That means the prerequisites and functionalities that are described here should only be considered when setting up email traffic for Toys Inc. in the SAP Solution Manager system (SAP Web AS 6.20). If you need information on the technical setup for sending SMS, fax, or pager, go to the SAP library at *http://help.sap.com*.

At Toys Inc., the central autoreaction method email is implemented for the BLA, BLN, and WAMA components in the SAP Solution Manager system.

SAPconnect

SAPconnect provides a standardized interface for external communication, which supports communication by telecommunication services such as fax, pager (SMS), Internet, and X400, as well as communication with printers and between several SAP systems. SAPconnect facilitates the connection of external communication components to the SAP system.

There are various options to link SAPconnect to an SAP system.

▶ **SAPconnect with RFC**

SAP's technology from Release 3.1 to 6.X allows for the connection of various gateways via RFC. These gateways transfer emails between the SAP system and a specified email server. That means they execute the actual email transfer via SMTP to or from remote participants. For example, email gateways can be the SAP Internet email gateway, SAP Exchange Connector, and also non-SAP products from partner companies.

▶ **SAPconnect with SMTP**

Using SAP Technology Release 6.10, the SAP system kernel directly supports SMTP (Internet email protocol). This means that no further components are necessary to send or receive email from the SAP system to each SMTP-compatible email server. This type of connection is described in the following section.

Setting the Autoreaction Method—Email via SMTP in Web AS 6.20

The following steps to set up the email autoreaction method through SMTP are described on the basis of the SAP Web Application Server Release 6.20. Furthermore, the setup refers only to outgoing email. You should note that deviations in the configuration can occur in other SAP releases.

In order to use the SMTP functionality, the profile must be compatible with SAP Web AS. Set the following profile parameters for SMTP. The <*> placeholder stands for a digit with which the parameters that can appear frequently can be numbered through consecutively, beginning with 0.

Maintain the parameter

```
icm/server_port_<*> = PROT=SMTP,PORT=<port>
```

in the SAP Solution Manager system. This opens a TCP/IP port to receive email through the SMTP plug-in. If you don't want to receive any email, set the port to 0.

Another parameter is

```
is/SMTP/virt_host_<*> = <host>:<port>,<port>,
...;.
```

Here a „virtual host" is defined for the receipt of email. This parameter is necessary only if several clients are to receive incoming email. If email is received and processed only in clients, this parameter is not necessary. We mention it here just for the sake of completing our discussion of this parameter. In our Toys Inc. example, it isn't relevant for the configuration.

The SAPconnect settings must be set up in the client that sends or receives email. Here you define, for example, which email server and port is used to send email from the system:

1 Call Transaction SCOT. Select the **View · System status** menu. The SMTP node can be found under the **INT** (Internet) element.
Each client contains exactly one SMTP node. It is automatically created by the system and cannot be deleted.

2 A double-click on the SMTP node takes you to the configuration screen (see Figure 4.25):

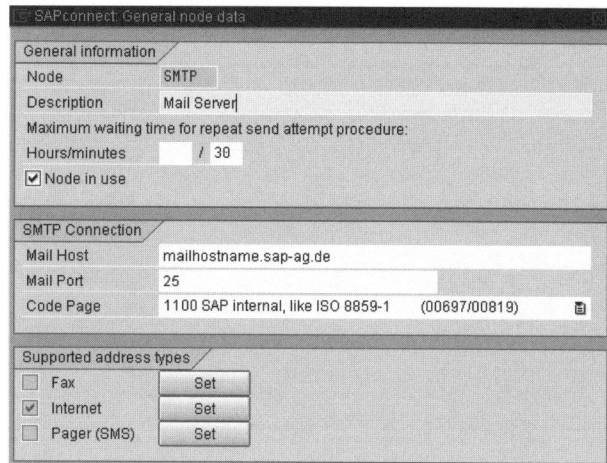

Figure 4.25 SAPconnect—General Node Data

3 Configure the SMTP node. In the **Hours/minutes** field, define in which time interval the connection must be re-established for the SMTP nodes if a temporary connection problem occurs.

4 Check the **Node in use** field.

5 Enter the email server in the **Mail Host** field and the corresponding port number in the **Mail Port** field.

6 Check the **Internet** field and click on the corresponding **Set** button. A new dialog opens.

7 Enter the address area of the recipient addresses that can be reached via this node. For instance, "*" (asterisk), if all email is to be sent via the SMTP node.

8 In **Output Formats for SAP Documents**, we recommend that you use the settings available in Figure 4.26.

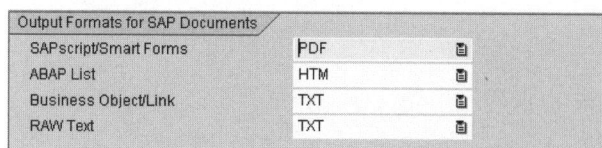

Figure 4.26 Output Formats for SAP Documents

9 You can decide whether you want a receipt confirmation for each outgoing email. By default, this functionality is deactivated. If you want to activate it, select the **Settings · Receipt Confirmation** menu. In our example, we'll limit ourselves to the standard **SAPconnect does not expect receipt confirm. for Internet mail** setting.

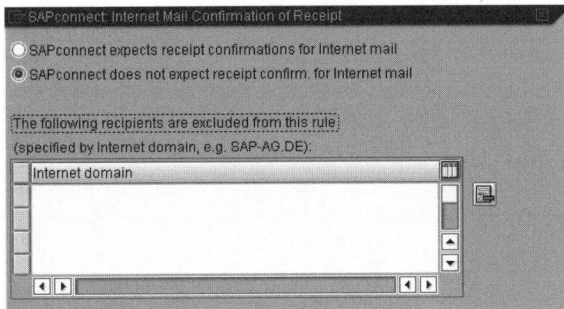

Figure 4.27 SAPconnect: Configuring the Internet Email Receipt Confirmation

Email sent from an SAP system is placed in a queue. A periodically scheduled background job, sent by SAPconnect jobsend, checks whether new email is in the queue and sends it, if necessary, from the queue. This job is scheduled in the SAP Solution Manager system by SAPconnect administration:

1 Call Transaction SCOT. Select **View · Jobs.** You can check here whether a send job is scheduled in SAPconnect. If you're not certain, you can also check **Simple Job selection in** Transaction SM37 to determine whether a job has already been scheduled in the RSCONN01 program.

2 Select **Job · Create.** A dialog opens.

3 Enter a name for the job here.

4 Confirm the entry with the **Enter** key or with the green check mark. Another dialog opens.

5 Select the **SAP&CONNECTALL** variant (see Figure 4.28).

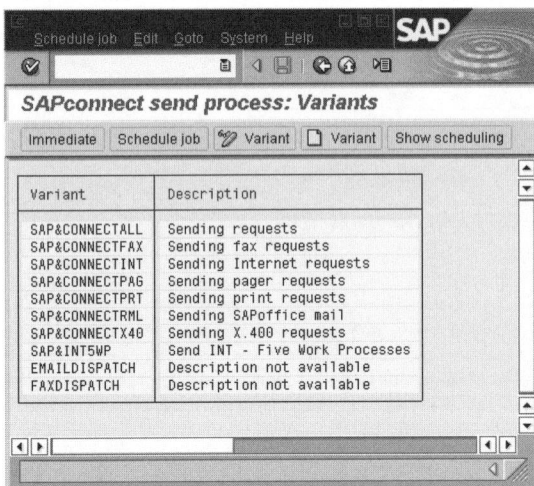

Figure 4.28 SAPconnect: Scheduling the Variant for the Send Process

6 Click on the **Schedule job** button. Another dialog opens.

7 In this dialog, click on the **Schedule periodically** button.

8 Set the time interval in which the job is started, for example, every five minutes, and confirm your entry with the **Create** button or the **Enter** key.

9 Use the **GoTo · Show scheduling menu** or the **Show scheduling** button to determine whether the job has been successfully created.

4.10 Central Autoreaction Methods

Since Basis Release 6.10, you can define central autoreaction methods in SAP components by using CCMS monitoring architecture. The autoreaction methods involved are not configured and started in the system in which the alert appears; rather, they are configured and started in the central monitoring system, which is an SAP Solution Manager system in our example. This means that work for setting up and changing autoreaction methods will be carried out at. The central monitoring system must have at least Basis Release 6.10, and the connected systems to be monitored must have the following or higher kernel status:

▶ 4.0B patchno 937
▶ 4.5B patchno 815
▶ 4.6B/C/D: from 4.6D patchno 1192
▶ 6.10 patchno 582
▶ 6.20 patchno 193

Furthermore, the SAPCCM4X agent is installed on every monitored SAP system and is connected with the central monitoring system.

SAP systems with Basis Release 3.1 (Release 3.1 requires the SAPCM3X agent) and systems that are centrally connected to SAPCCMSR agents are automatically part of the central monitoring system. Therefore, the autoreaction methods are always started centrally.

Setting Up the Central Autoreaction Method

The configuration of the central autoreaction method is carried out in the SAP Solution Manager system.

1 Call Transaction RZ21. Select **Technical Infrastructure · Assign Central Autoreactions.** You have entered the **Manage Central Autoreactions** screen (see Figure 4.29).

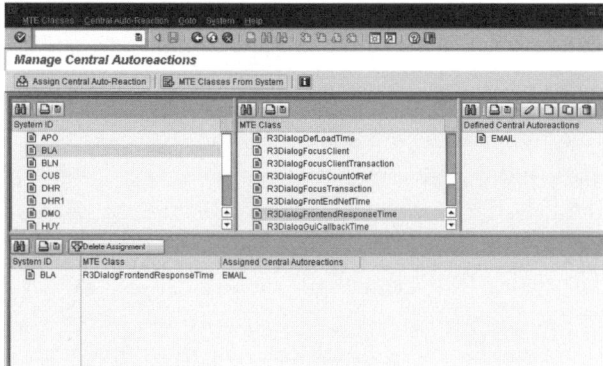

Figure 4.29 Managing Central Autoreactions

The screen is split into four areas. In the upper left-hand **System ID** area, you can see the systems that are connected to the central monitoring system. In the central area, there is a selection of MTE classes. On the right-hand side, you can see the central auto-reactions, which you define by assigning systems to the relevant MTE class. In the bottom area, you get an overview of assignments already stored.

2 Define a central autoreaction method. You can do this either through the **Create centr. Autoreaction** menu or via the **Defined Central Autoreactions** pane and click on the **Create** button. A new dialog opens.

3 Enter your preferred method name into the field next to the **Create** button. Then, click on the **Create** button.

  Alternatively, you can also execute an existing autoreaction method centrally. Enter the existing method into the entry field next to the **Create with template** button, and click on this button. The new **Monitoring: Methods** dialog opens.

4 Enter the corresponding method settings. Note the following settings in the respective tabs:

  ▶ **Execution**
    Enter the report or the function module to be executed. If you like, you can use the SALO_EMAIL_IN_CASE_OF_ALERT function module provided by SAP.

  ▶ **Control**
    Select **only in central system, triggered by CCMS agents.**

  ▶ **Parameters**
    Enter the sender, recipient, and address type.

  ▶ **Release**
    Mark the **Autoreaction method** field.

5 Save your entries.

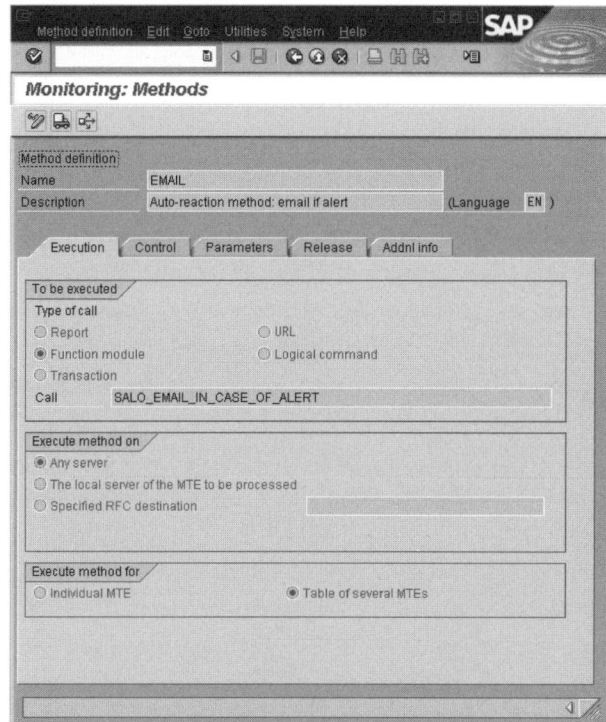

Figure 4.30 Setting the Autoreaction Method

Assigning the Central Autoreaction Method

1 Call Transaction RZ21. Select **Assign Central Autoreactions** from the **Technical Infrastructure** menu. You are now in the **Manage Central Autoreactions** dialog screen.

2 Select the systems in the **System ID** area to be included in the central autoreaction methods and the MTE class that you want to include in the **MTE Class** area.

3 Select the desired autoreaction method in the **Defined Central Autoreactions** area, which you would like to assign to the marked classes and the marked systems.

4 Click on the **Assign Central Auto-Reaction** button. In the **System ID** pane, you will now see the corresponding assignment.

Carry out the steps until you have assigned all the desired autoreaction methods to the corresponding systems and the desired MTE class.

Activating Central System Dispatching

Once you have defined and assigned the autoreaction methods, you can activate the central system dispatching.

You are still in Transaction RZ21. Select **Techn. Infrastructure · Method Execution · Activate Central System Dispatching**.

Ensure that you start the central autoreaction methods under the user name in the client that was activated by the central method dispatcher. If you use the automatic alert notification, the client is crucial. After activation, ensure that you are in the client from which email is to be sent.

Parameter Maintenance of the Autoreaction Method Email

Autoreaction methods such as email can be assigned to an MTE class. If an alarm is triggered for the MTE according to first values, the SAP system automatically sends an email to the specified recipient. Three important pieces of information are necessary for this:

► **Sender**
The sender is an SAP user name in whose name the email is sent. This user must be available in Client 000. An email address must be assigned to this user.

► **Recipient**
The recipient can be an Internet address or a mailing list.

► **ID Sender Type (Address type)**
The sender or address type is dependent on the sender. The sender determines the method of communication. If you send an email to an Internet address, the corresponding address type is "U". Possible recipient types with the related address type are listed in Table 4.9.

Recipient type	Example	Address type
SAP user name	Muser	B
External address	Mary Miller	A
General mailing list	Monitoring team	C
Internet address	mary.miller	U

Table 4.9 Recipient Types with the Corresponding Address Type

Monitoring the External Transmission Processes

Transmission processes that come from the central monitoring system can be checked in the **Administration of external transmissions** monitor. According to a defined time-frame, which you specify, you can display all transmission processes:

1 Call Transaction SOST. You are now in the **Administration of external transmissions** monitor (see Figure 4.31).

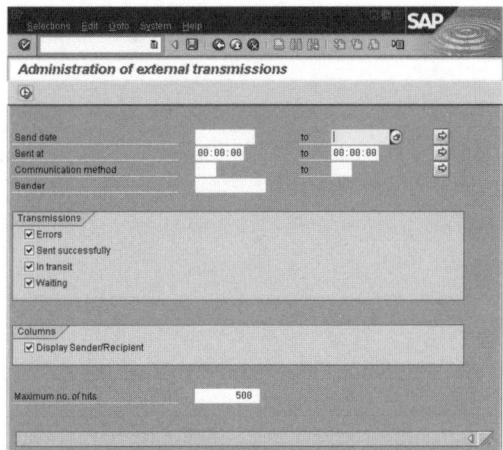

Figure 4.31 Overview of External Transmissions

2 Define the time range in the **Send date** and the **Sent at** fields for which you want to see the transmission processes.

3 Optionally, you can select the type of communication in the **Communication method** and **Sender** fields.

4 Select which transmission status you would like displayed. You can choose among the following: **Errors**, **Sent successfully**, **In transit**, and **Waiting**.

5 Activate or deactivate the **Display Sender/Recipient** field.

6 Click on the **Execute** button or the **F8** key. A new dialog opens that displays an overview of the external transmissions.

5 Final Considerations

Throughout the practice sections of this book, you have done more than simply implement a monitoring system in SAP Solution Manager; you have ventured forth into the area of centralized system monitoring. The implementation and configuration of system monitoring in SAP Solution Manager was successfully achieved through precise and meticulous preparation. This required our need to distinguish system monitoring and other functional areas, as well as selecting system components, from their monitoring components. With the use of our example company, Toys Inc., you learned what we need to focus on during the conceptual phase of the project, while developing a monitoring concept. You also learned what activities are necessary to successfully implement the monitoring concept in SAP Solution Manager.

You should not be under the misconception that upon completing the practice examples your work is done. It is now up to you to test the system monitoring solution that has been implemented. By using typical testing examples or scenarios, which you have experimented with throughout the course of your work, you can simulate possible system problems. This also means that you should not only test whether various monitoring objects set off alarms or autoreaction methods; you also need to recreate troubleshooting and escalation procedures. Specifically, you must ensure that the processes are harmonious and that they can be easily managed by current employees. The best process description is not particularly useful if the people responsible are not available, or if there isn't sufficient know-how to solve a specific problem. The area of problem resolution, in particular, can be merged with actual administrative tasks.

After a successful test phase and once the central system monitoring is in operation, another phase in the follow-up work begins—the optimization of your system monitoring model. In this context, we recommend that you check alarms triggered by individual monitoring objects that have been implemented, in accordance with their threshold value definitions. Often, you will find that threshold values have been set too low and therefore an alarm is triggered prematurely by exceeding or falling below the value. In this case, you can infer that the alarm triggered is not a real indicator of the system status. Here, you should also check whether sufficient autoreaction methods have been defined for individual monitoring objects. Perhaps there are still one or more objects that require an autoreaction method. Or, maybe you think that a system component could be better integrated into the monitoring system, although this didn't appear to be the case at the start.

As you can see, there is no one monitoring concept that applies to all system landscapes. It is not only the different IT landscapes that make the concept non-transferable, but also the differing views on system monitoring held by individual people. Each person has an individual reason why he or she regards something as being important in system monitoring. This very point is what makes it so essential that the person responsible for a project is someone who can use his or her system monitoring experience to provide better insight into the value of monitoring individual objects. There are some general rules that you can adhere to in system monitoring. But, apart from this, each system can be adapted according to the specific conditions of individual systems.

We hope that this book has not only reinforced the necessity of a centralized monitoring system, but has also highlighted the work inherent in introducing system monitoring and its multiple uses.

Index

ISBN 1-59229-053-1

1st edition 2005, 1st reprint 2006

© 2005 by Galileo Press GmbH
SAP PRESS is an imprint of Galileo Press,
Fort Lee (NJ), USA
Bonn, Germany

Translation Lemoine International, Inc., Salt Lake City, UT
Copy Editor Nancy Etscovitz, UCG, Inc., Boston, MA
Cover Design Vera Brauner
Printed in Germany